AF230290

THE HUMAN STORY

THE
HUMAN
STORY

Roger B. Lane, Ph.D.

Limited First Edition Published by Soundly, Inc. in October 2023
Copyright © 2024 by Roger B. Lane, Ph.D.

Designed by Amy Blank
Cover by Amy Blank and Lara Saget

For information contact: Soundly, Inc., 229 East 85 St. #1347, New York, NY 10028

ISBN: 978-0-9985610-0-4

Printed in the United States of America

*For the Soul Present with my grandson Vincent James Lane
and for all Souls, Travelers all*

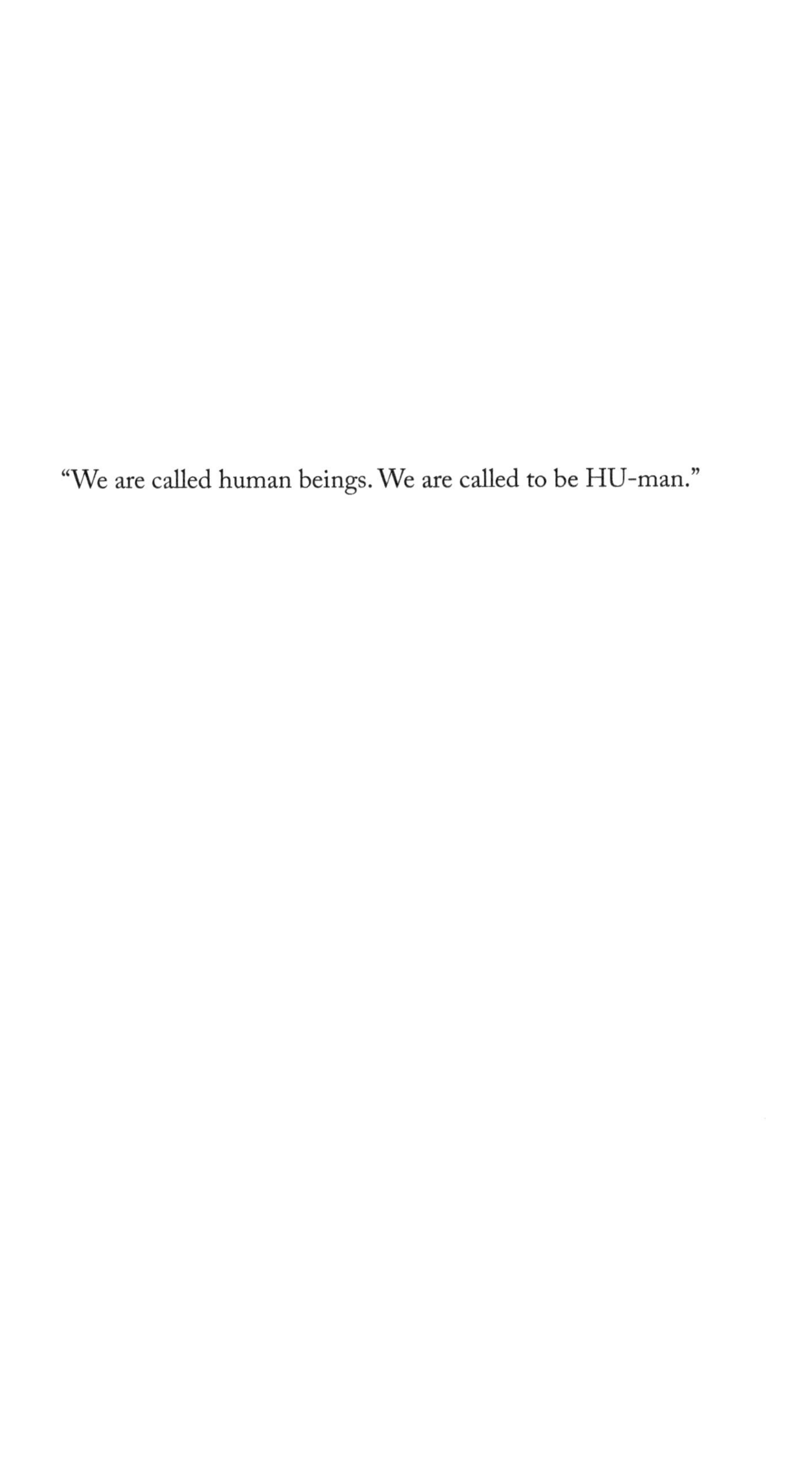

"We are called human beings. We are called to be HU-man."

TABLE OF CONTENTS

PREFACE

As a child about to enter my teenage years I stood in the House of Worship and, moved by the music and prayers, tried to pierce the stone building as if I were a superhero with laser beams for eyes so that I would see God and not feel separate and having to connect.

A few years later I realized that what we see in people is really within ourSelves and that we are simply unaware that It is within us. Taking this to its logical conclusion, I realized that my burning desire to see God could only be because of the simple fact that, up until then, I was unaware that God was within me.

But where? What is the access point? Is an access point even needed as God could be right there in me?

Concomitant with this, my interest in approaches to God blossomed and I read voraciously about the different approaches—whether in ancient Egypt or Mesoamerica; the Eastern ones found in India and Southeast Asia and the

Islamic ones found throughout the recent Muslim world; the Judeo-Christian approaches, including the heterodox ones of the Gnostics and as expressed in the Books of the Apocrypha as well as in Spiritual Movements and histories of religion and religious beliefs.

I began to see that everything is, quite simply, inside out and backwards.

I began to understand that it wasn't a question of "connecting" with God or reaching God because the simple Truth is that God is within but rather of Allowing Its Unfolding.

I had also fine-tuned the location question of where God is: It was no longer necessary to reach God within as there was no separation, not only from the outside, but also from the inside. I began to have the inkling that God was, quite simply, immediate as He was living in me as me.

The issue for me now became to turn this inkling into Knowing. This Knowing came into fruition with my introduction into a Sound Current Path. I Learned that it is not a question of powering oneSelf to God but, rather just the opposite: of Allowing the layers of karmic gauze to be peeled away much like the layers of an onion and much like a person who is thirsty needs to cup gently the water rather than grab it.

As I grew in understanding I saw the necessity of helping people who struggled with the same central issue of letting go of our minds and emotions and founded Cosmos Tree in 1978, which during the years has helped many thousands of Souls in Classes and Workshops and, as I grew Spiritually in the Knowledge that Tag! We are It! I founded in 1992 the Center For Religion And Advanced Spiritual Studies to help Souls Walk the Path Of Soul Transcendence according to the New Dispensation as described in the book. The

Center's acronym—CRASS—indicates that The Process is, indeed, inside out and backwards from the usual norms.

Throughout my involvement with and the studying of different approaches to God I was always struck by the use of food as part of the religious rituals and festivals, ceremonies and the Reality of what I call the Inner Banquet.

This has led me to present <u>The Human Story</u> as a meal with Appetizers, Entrées and Desserts. The Appetizers to whet your appetite and appreciation, the Entrées to both satiate and fuel the fire of Knowing yourSelf and the Desserts so that the Experiences are sweet ones.

I realize that I can only present the Map of ourSelves as Spirit and that it is up to the Reader to Travel this Road and partake of the Divine Caterer's Feast.

I Lovingly Encourage you to do so.

It is, indeed, the Soul's Blueprint.

ACKNOWLEDGEMENTS

There are many people I wish to thank who helped to shape and form this book so I will start my acknowledgement of them and my sincere appreciation at the beginning.

Before there was a book there was a question. Thank you, Peggy Heatherly, for asking me the question, "When are you going to write another book?"

While this question kicked off the formation of a book of The Teachings Of The Path Of Soul Transcendence That I am Blessed to Bring Forth it took the repeat of this question to give it physical form. Thank you, Jim Thompson, for asking this question again. And thank you to those who donated to the Center For Religion And Advanced Spiritual Studies in recognition of the importance of bringing This Project to fruition.

To help pair the Tools That help to Understand and Apply The Teachings and to highlight The Teachings That stand out a team that I dubbed the "I-Squad" was formed that Jim also captained. The work of Its members—Marilyn

Fiala, Howard Grossman, Melissa Sones, Nancy Rand, Amy Blank, Lara Saget, Valentina Isleib, and Jim—helped to give this book much flavor, for which I am grateful.

I was able to discuss the actual process of writing with my son Jeffrey who, as a sociologist, is the author of several books and of many scholarly articles and who taught me about writing blocs. When I mentioned that I wished to use footnotes to be educational on the subject rather than just a note about the author and publisher and pages of the material used, Jeffrey suggested Endnotes instead, which I happily followed. Thank you, Jeffrey, for your invaluable help.

To help give the book form a manuscript was needed and Amy Blank typed it through its many rounds and provided very useful comments to make the book intelligible to all readers. Melissa Sones provided excellent copyediting skills to give the book stylistic consistency and continuance. Thank you, Amy and Melissa, for being the nuts and bolts of bringing this to book form. All errors are mine and mine alone.

And thank you again, Amy, for your collaboration and expertise with the book design that ensures an aesthetically pleasing experience while reading. And thank you again, Amy and Lara Saget, for a very appetizing and delicious cover.

And a big "thank you" to my wife of many years, Anna, for just being there with her companionship and helpful advice; cooking and love.

And, lastly, to the Spirit we all *are* That sustains us and That Brought Forth The Teachings Presented in This Book and That is, in Reality, The Teachings and This Book.

A Note On The Text

A capital letter within a word—such as ourSelves—refers to the Divine that we *are* within the container of our bodies. A capital letter not normally capitalized represents an aspect or quality of the Divine or the Divine Itself as do those in a phrase.

FIRST COURSE

Context

It is very important that proper context be given to the Spiritual Action now enveloping Humankind.

We *are* Souls. We *are* Spirit. That is the Simple Truth of Our Existence. We have forgotten Our True Nature and, as a result, are subject to be at the effect of what we have put in motion with our identification with our thoughts and feelings. This improper identification with our thoughts and feelings is the separation from ourSelves as Soul, as Spirit and results in what is commonly called karma and reincarnation.

This karma and reincarnation—also known as the Wheel of 84—is partially why we are wearing a body now and have many times before and why we may very well need to again.

We, as Soul, are Powerful Creators and are Responsible for what we have created by our identifying with our thoughts and feelings. These thoughts and feelings that we have persisted in become creations that become lodged between ourSelves and the Spirit we *are*.

Where are they lodged? That question was answered very eloquently a few thousand years ago: "In my Father's house are many mansions." This well-known quote from the New Testament means that there are many Realms or Levels in Spirit or in the Inner Worlds. These Realms or Levels are differentiated from one another by Their Frequencies or the density of matter that resides on that particular Level or, conversely, how much Spirit resides on Each.

There is a demarcation point—the Soul Realm—"below" Which, with very rare exceptions, a Soul is subject to this Wheel of 84 and at Which the Soul is free from this cycle of birth and death. This in the West is Known as Eternal Life.

It is important to note that a Soul—despite the claims of many religions—does not Enter Eternal Life simply because It is no longer wearing a body.

It is easier to understand this if we view the body as the Housing or container for the Soul That we, in fact, *are*. When the Soul leaves the body—described in the spiritual literature of the East as the cutting of the silver cord—the body is no longer animated and can no longer function and is "dead". But it is the body that is dead and not us.

Yes! We are more than our thoughts and feelings and our body. We are more than our material self living in this world.

This truth has a very wonderful implication: if we are more than our material self then we are nonmaterial as well and, if we can know ourSelves materially through our senses, then we can Know ourSelves nonmaterially—other than through the senses—as Soul, as the Spirit we *are*.

The question then becomes how is This possible? How can we Know ourSelves as Soul, as Spirit? How can we Know ourSelves as the nonmaterial Beings we *are* while living in the material world, the world of form?

Many people coming to Know themSelves—beyond the psychological self—run into this dilemma and then discard this Sacred Process because they are not aware of how to Know themSelves other than through the senses. Or people discard the Living Reality of the Divine Oscillation—commonly called God—because It is reduced to materiality—an anthropomorphic father figure—and to a "concept"—as something in which to believe rather than a Living Reality—or to an "ideal"—something to which to aspire but impossible to reach unless you are a saint.

Nothing is further from the Truth. God—The Divine Oscillation—has Given us a Way! This Way is Known as Initiation Into The Sound Current.

The Sound Current is known by many names and found in many religions. It is the Word in the Bible and called Sant-i-Surmad by the Sufis. In the Holy Book of the Sikhs—the Adi Granth—it is called the Nam and Muslims know It as Kalma in the Koran. It is known as Shabd in Hindi.

This is the Audible Life Stream, the Creative Power Itself.

We, as Souls, are Created from This and as This. The Great Oversoul—referred to as God or the Lord, God—*is* This, and we, as Souls, are Created of and as this Same Essence. This is What is referred to by the Bible as "created in God's Image".

This Audible Life Stream can be heard by the Soul after It has been Initiated by The Master and engages in Its Spiritual Progression.

As mentioned earlier, there are many Realms or Frequencies upon Which the Soul lives. These Levels or Frequencies lie dormant until They are Stirred Awake at The Time Of Initiation and the person providing the Housing for the Soul is Taught The Proper Method to go into the Soul Body and Know Itself as Soul, as Spirit. For, as the Soul

Progresses and gains Spiritual Power, the Soul is *conscious* of each of the Realms It is Awake on; in other words, as It Progresses It can hold the Frequencies of These Realms.

This is how the Soul Comes to Know Itself as Soul, as Spirit, as, in fact, the Living God.

God, in His Kindness and Mercy, has Given us—through this Process of Initiation Into The Sound Current—the Opportunity to explore and enjoy His "House"—the Realms and Frequencies of the Inner Worlds—That are His Manifestation.

The above serves to give you a basic contextual understanding of Reality. And it is also important to give you a historical context for the Spiritual Movement now taking place.

The "Death of God" Movement began in the nineteenth century, coining the phrase used by Fredrick Nietzsche. This was a summation of the movement began in the Enlightenment that highlighted and developed the primacy of reason over faith and continued into the twentieth century with the Holocaust offering the final "proof".

Whether the Death of God is taken literally that God has died or that transcendence has, it is easy to see that the world has become more secularized and that many more of its inhabitants experience being adrift and without purpose.

God/Spirit/The Divine Oscillation—Whatever you wish to call It—has been pushed to the margins rather than "central" to Our Being when, in fact, It *is* Our Being.

Spirit has Given us another Opportunity to Remedy the plight of modern humanity. It needs to be noted that, both individually and collectively, Spirit does not violate Our Free Will and so we will need to Choose into This.

What is the Remedy?

Before this question can be answered we need to

understand an essential fact about Spirit. Most of us, when we think of the Inner Worlds of Spirit, either go blank or envision a man with a long beard wearing a flowing robe residing there. In either case, we think of the Spirit as being finished. While Creation is finished in the lower worlds[1]— Those Realms or Levels Where the Soul is still subject to karma and reincarnation—It is not in the Levels of Spirit beyond those of form, where there is density.

It is important to note that of These Worlds of Pure Spirit located *within* us as Soul, as Spirit, the Level Vibrating at the Highest Frequency—besides the Unmanifested One— is Known as HU, The First Manifestation of God.

This tells us Our True Nature. The human race is quite simply, HU-man Beings, Manifestations of the Lord, God.

In other words, Tag we're It!

In contradistinction to creation being unfinished and still going on in the Inner Worlds of Spirit, there is the Absolute. This Divine Oscillation, commonly called God or the Godhead, is the only unchanging and unchangeable Reality. This may prove to be off-putting and offensive in this age where everything is relative and of equal importance but, nevertheless, It is the Truth.

What has changed is our approach to God that is reflected in religions, theologies and in spiritual movements. Religions, theologies and these spiritual movements demonstrate our Growth in Consciousness.

This Growth in Consciousness is different from that thought of by the general population and different from that taught in major universities. Rather than be equated with memory of the mind's awareness of itself and its environs, Consciousness is Spirit as the Fulfillment of Itself by Its Engagement and Completion of Its Knowledge of Itself:

Knowing Itself as Soul, as Spirit; in fact, the Living God.

The history of these movements in the last few thousand years can very briefly be summed up as a movement from fear of the environment and living to being in control of it by having a totem to control the environment; to each aspect of god being considered a god; to incorporating them into a few gods and then into one or, in some of the eastern religions, into an invisible force running through it all.

This Movement in Consciousness then reflects what I call the "location question". Where is this One? The One moves from having created the world and then removing Itself to being in the world as reflected in the Spiritual Movement that focuses on the Sound Current, to being able as Soul to "hook up" or join the Divine—of which It is a part—That exists outside Itself.

And now is the Time for a further Growth In Consciousness.

What is This Growth In Consciousness and Why is It necessary? In order to begin to answer this very important question we must first explore the meaning of the word "religion" and its field of activity.

"Religion" is defined generally as the belief in and worship of a superhuman controlling power, especially, a personal God or gods. From this it is easy to see that the belief embodies the notion that God or the gods lie above and beyond us. With this viewpoint we need a "middleman"—whether it be clergy, a Redeemer or a rare saint—who can bridge this "gap". We also see that this figure is anthropomorphic; that is "human", however "super".

We also need to take a closer look at why this "gap" exists. It is a psychological truth that whatever we as "human" beings cannot accept within ourSelves we project onto others. Here we cannot Accept our own Divinity so It gets projected onto this figure in the sky.

Why can't we Accept ourSelves as Divine? The answer is reflected in many theologies: we are "sinners"; "have fallen"; "do not merit", etc. These theological thoughts and verdicts are based upon our feelings towards ourSelves and the simple fact that Earth is a part of the dual or lower worlds.

What happens in the dual worlds is that there are two poles—the negative and the positive—that manifest this planet and all the lower worlds. These negative and positive poles are neither "bad" nor "good"—but are simply denoted as negative and positive to connote the type of charge it carries; this is just as the two polarities of a battery.

There is always separation between these poles in duality. Similarly, the same mechanism of separation is found in psychology. It is only through a process of psychological maturation that an individual can incorporate "good" and "bad" within themSelves. Usually, the "bad" is projected onto others—whether individuals, groups or nations—with the result often being war.

This seeming "separation" though has an underlying cause and it is a simple one. We, as Souls, embodied to have an Experience Of Creation and when we were Created we were Given Free Will—the Power to Choose. We Exercised this Free Will to choose away from ourSelves as Spirit, as Soul and a "separation" resulted. We did this by identifying with our thoughts and feelings in our existences in the world of form. This "separation" is generally known as karma.

This "problem" of karma and its cause contains its solution and its dissolution.

Since karma is created by our identification with our thoughts and feelings or, as we have been taught, "whatever we focus upon we become"[2] we can Choose other than into this improper identification. We can Choose into What I call Proper Identification or, in short, Proper ID.

What is Proper ID? As mentioned earlier we are wearing a body partially because we have falsely identified with our thoughts and feelings while previously in the world of form and we are at the effect of this in the present body we are inhabiting. If this, however, is only a partial reason then what is the other part?

The other part of the reason we are here is because we have been Given a special and Grand Opportunity: the Opportunity to Know ourSelves as Soul, as Spirit, as, in fact, the Living God.

If we have been Given this Wonderful Opportunity then it stands to reason that we must be exactly What we are to discover about ourSelves. We must be Soul; we must be Spirit. We must be, in Reality, the very Manifestation of the Lord, God. Simply put, God lives in us as us.

Once again, it is easier to understand this if we see the body as a container for the Soul, for the Spirit That *is* God. If we identify with the body and its accompanying thoughts and feelings then we are practicing improper ID. Practicing Proper ID is to identify ourSelves as Spirit, as Soul, Which, in turn, allows us to move beyond the mechanistic operation of karma—however true—into the Wonderful Knowing and understanding that HU-man Life is a Gift, a Wonderful and rare Opportunity to Know yourSelf as God.

How can we truly Know This beyond Its being a "concept" or "construct"—and beyond mental comprehension with its limitations?

This book spends the following pages answering this question and bringing to the reader the sense of Wonder and Awe That reside *within*.

Meaning and Purpose

It is important to note that This Opportunity called HU-man Life is *inherent* in It and not derived from or as a result of an existential quest for meaning and purpose.

Life in general may seem like a big ball of wax with no ultimate meaning and purpose other than its just being and one's individual life may seem the same.

We live in an age of relativism—cognitively, ethically, aesthetically—which does not permit the existence of an Absolute. In the small confines in which an absolute is still permitted to exist it is always outside the field of action and is seen as imposed upon the actor and, thus, a target against which to rebel.

This thing called HU-man Life is theologically perceived as where the Infinite touches into the finite. Once again, the Absolute—in this case the Infinite or God or Spirit—is perceived as located outside of the field of action, making inroads into it. It is, in fact, taken as basically separate and as a distinct entity.

What about if we Practiced Proper ID with our viewpoint of HU-man Life? If, instead of identifying with the finite, we see it from the Spiritual Viewpoint? What about just as Spirit or God lives *within* us as us, the Infinite lives within the finite as "finite"?

If we take this Spiritual Viewpoint of Oneness then it is easy to see that the Infinite motivates and serves as the "motor" for the finite.

What has made the separation seem so very real that it felt like it could never be leapt over let alone discovered that it really does not exist?

It is our collective creations away from the Spirit we *are*—karma, as described earlier—that have created this illusion of separateness. What each Soul has done on an individual level is done collectively and this greatly muddies the waters of our perception.

In addition, most Souls living in the world of form do not have *direct access* to Spirit so They can only Know the Infinite —Spirit or the Lord, God—by reflection.

When we see pebbles at the bottom of a lake, for instance, they seem to be in one place but, if we dive to retrieve them, we will miss them as they are not where they seem to be.

We, similarly, miss the mark in our approach to God. Our thoughts about God—our theologies—are NOT God; they are thoughts about God, about a God located outside ourSelves—even though the Infinite may be on this planet— and separate from ourSelves.

A person doesn't need to be a physicist to understand and to know intuitively that we cannot accurately know through our senses. It is much like the Heisenberg Uncertainty Principle: the observer disturbs the observed. Even keeping the illusion of separation "real"—with God on one hand, the human race on the other—we cannot Know ourSelves nor God through the senses.

Atheists and agnostics base their "reasoning" upon this: since we cannot see God It doesn't exist or we cannot see or Know God so how do we know It exists.

This reasoning is incomplete and based upon a faulty assumption and that is that we can only know through our senses.

Religious believers face a similar dilemma: their God is outside of themSelves and is the object of their belief or, if within, a connection needs to be made. There is no Knowing, only various degrees of conviction based upon tradition, fear, idealism or many other personal and cultural factors.

This gap, this separation between Humankind and the Divine Oscillation—the Lord, God or Spirit or The Great Oversoul—is, in fact, the grand illusion of HU-man Life.

How does an individual rise above this illusion that seemingly governs HU-man Life? Before this extremely important question can be answered we need to pay a short visit to religions.[1]

Religions, like all things, do not operate in a vacuum. They were mainly formed from the *zeitgeist* of the times for purposes of controlling the world around it or to bring law and order in a society or idealism or moral law to it.

The separation or, at best, the Divine Spark within reflected in these religions reflects, as previously noted, the consciousness of the time. One filled with creations— thoughts and emotions—away from the Divine or, in other words, karma.

Religions, thus, use symbols to represent the Divine— whether the Five Books of Moses (Torah), bread and wine or statues and idols. This is akin to going to a restaurant for a delicious meal and eating the menu.

And in some cases the existence of God—the basis of the religion being formed—was deduced from dreams.

This practice, where the one seeking to be healed from a malady—physical, mental or emotional—would go to a Sacred Cave and the priest/healer would dream the remedy for that person, lends us to another definition of "religion"—religion is from the word "religio" meaning to "link back".[2] We are able to rise above the seeming reality of separation by "linking back" to What and Who we *are*.

If we are more than our physical body—and by Practicing Proper Identification we Know this—then there must be an "apparatus" beyond the physical that provides the means for this "link back".

This nonmaterial "apparatus" is the Soul, also called the Soul Body. It is *within* all individuals but lies dormant, awaiting Its Awakening through Its many incarnations.

How does this Awakening of the Soul happen? Is it by happenstance, luck or is It gratuitous with no rhyme or reason?

At the Spiritually Correct Time the Soul Present With the HU-man Receives Initiation from The Master Soul Who is often referred to as The Teacher or Guru or simply, Sound Current Master. The Soul is Quickened and the Sound Current or Holy Spirit That has lain dormant is Sparked Awake by The Master's Grace. The Meditation Technique is also Imparted At This Time Of Initiation to enable the Initiate to go into the Soul Body and be with the Lord, God. As noted earlier there are many Levels That the Soul lives on—"in My Father's House are many mansions"—and Those Souls on the Levels below the Soul Realm are subject to karma and reincarnation or the Wheel of 84. Through following *exactly* the Meditation Technique Given by The Teacher At This Time Of Initiation, the Soul goes through These Realms, as It can Hold and Maintain the Frequency of Each of These Realms or Levels.

A Soul That has Entered What's called Eternal Life is able to be with God because It has the Spiritual Strength to Hold the Frequency of the Soul Realm, not just because It has dropped Its Housing in a process called "death".

It needs to be noted that there are many Levels between the Soul Realm and the Unmanifested One and, with very few exceptions, Initiates were not able to continue while in the body with Their Spiritual Progression past the Soul Realm.

It also needs to be noted that Souls reincarnate[3] from any of Those Realms below the Soul Realm. As Souls are in different stages of Their Spiritual Progression, the Classroom—the Same One That is The Wonderful Opportunity to Fulfill the Purpose of HU-man Life—called the Earth has many grades. Just as we do not judge a fifth grader for not being in the tenth grade we cannot judge Souls for not being "further along".

The key point is that *every* Soul here—with the very rare exception of a Master Soul, as an Expression of Divine Love, Incarnating out of Its Choice to assist HU-mankind in Its Spiritual Progression—is doing Its Progression. Its Progression in the "long" Life of the Soul here is One of Upliftment and Growth, of Upvibration. This holds true for Souls That are uninitiated and "just" here for the Opportunity to balance karma.

We need to understand the importance of the Housing for the Soul. You may have noted that it was said that "the Soul Present with the HU-man Received Initiation ..." as It is the Soul That is Initiated and NOT the person; It is the nonmaterial "apparatus" That comes front and center.

What is the role of the conscious part of ourSelves? It is to direct Our Focus to The Spirit We *Are*. It is to direct Our Focus into This rather than to allow our attention to be pulled out into our karma by the part of ourSelves[4] that carries our karmic patterns.

When we have completely come to Know that the "object" of Our Focus and ourSelves is One and The Same—It is all Love, all God—then we have gone to Completion here and the individual Soul loses Its identity as a unique Soul and is merged with the Godhead and, as noted earlier, generally may not continue Its Spiritual Progression in the body.

Much like reincarnation does not take away from the importance of our present incarnation but enhances it because of the increased importance of how we Exercise Our Free Will and the choices we make and the resulting Foci so, too, does the fact that It is the Soul That has been Initiated and not the wearer of the body increase the importance of being in the body and of the wearer.

This "link back" to What and Who we *are*—the Living God—is *within* us and *is* What and Who we *are*. In other words, we are linking back to Ourselves. We have forgotten Who and What we *are* because of our choices away from the Spirit we *are*.

God in His Kindness and Mercy has provided us with the Divine Remedy. Since we have forgotten Who and What we *are* we are Given the Opportunity to Remember This through Initiation Into The Sound Current.

Since this "memory" is not of the mind but lies in the Spirit we *are*, well beyond the linking of consciousness with memory as taught in major universities—it must be Stirred Awake in the Soul At The Time Of Initiation. Just like being stirred completely awake out of bed is a gradual process so, too, is the Complete Awakening of the Soul.

By following this Process *exactly* as Taught At The Time Of Initiation the Initiated Soul Remembers Itself—

It becomes again Aware of Itself—and has Consciousness beyond the mind's memory with the selectivity and limitation and distortions of the lower realms.

As noted before, the Soul lives on many Levels. When the Soul has Entered into being Fully Awake It has Simultaneous Awareness of *all* the Levels It lives on. Until such time, the Soul has Awareness of the Level It is Awake on and all Those below It as It continues Its Journey through the Realms. The Higher the Frequency It can Hold the more Awareness It has as It increases the Frequencies or Realms It Holds.

As noted earlier, the Soul comes to Know that It, the "object" of Its Love—the Divine Oscillation or Living God—and the Love "between" Them are One and The Same. Since this Divine Oscillation Lives *within* us as us doesn't it stand the test of reason that we are Awakening to Ourselves, to the simple fact that we *are* This Divine Oscillation, the Living God—a fact that we have obscured by our choices away from That Which we *are*, resulting in separation or karma as it is known?

Although we have separated ourSelves from the Spirit we *are* and have forgotten Ourselves through these choices, the Purpose of Our Original Creation As Soul—"in the beginning was the Word and the Word was with God"[5]—remains the same.

What was this Purpose? Souls were Created to Experience Creation and the Creator, to Know the Living God and the Creations made.

This Meaning and Purpose of HU-man Life continues today, Its Intention unaltered.

You will have noticed that the Purpose of Our Original Creation is to Experience Creation and you will have Learned that This Creation, while It includes the earth and the physical world and the lower Inner Worlds, also includes many more

Levels in the Spiritual Worlds so that Our Experiencing Creation involves Levels beyond the worlds of form.

How can we Know This Divine Oscillation That lives beyond these worlds of form? We Know This through the Gift Of Initiation Into The Sound Current.

If the Purpose of HU-man Life is to experience the Living God and all of Creation and Creation extends well beyond the worlds of form then it is plain to see that HU-man Life is the Blessed Opportunity to Fulfill This Purpose and that the Lord, God in His Kindness and Mercy has Provided the Way: Initiation Into The Sound Current or Holy Spirit.

New Paradigm: Tag! You're It!

Taking a look at all the theistic religions—those in which there is something called God involved—we see an evolution of Where God is located and in Our Relationship To God.

It is to our advantage to take a look at the reason for this seeming change in location of the Godhead. As noted earlier, It has gone from standing outside Creation to being in It to being involved with the Universe to being here on the planet—even if through an "agent" such as a Messiah or Holy Spirit—to being *within* us.

As we have discussed earlier, when talking about the psychological principle of projection, whatever we cannot accept within ourSelves gets projected outside of ourSelves. As God did not hire a moving van and change addresses nor conquer a different continent, when we look at religious history as the history of HU-man Consciousness we understand why the location of What is called God has seemingly changed.

As HU-man Beings have grown in Consciousness the Divine *within* has become more and more accepted and less and less projected outside until, at the cutting edge of This Advance in Consciousness, the Divine is located in Its Proper Place; that is, *within* each of us.

We see here the veracity and the importance of What is called The First Law Of Spirit.[1] It is, quite simply, Acceptance.

Just as HU-man Consciousness has evolved to locate the Divine *within* so, too, has It evolved in Its relationship with God. Many current Spiritual Groups have the proper location for God—*within*—and teach that Our Purpose is to connect to It by the Practice Given At Initiation.

But to "connect" implies a separateness that needs to be joined or linked together, that needs to be bridged.

The New Paradigm is the next step in HU-man Consciousness That is available now.

What is this next step that is appearing now? In order to answer and appreciate it, we need to remember an extremely important definition: the definition of the Christed Consciousness. We also need to remember that It is the definition of a Consciousness that is *within* each of us and not that of a religion or a religious figure that is easily dismissed. The definition, as stated earlier, is that Our Will and God's Will are One and The Same. It then stands to reason that we *are* One and The Same as God and simply need to Wake up to this fact.

Practicing The First Law Of Spirit—Acceptance—we Accept that we *are* One and The Same. This is the next step in Our Relationship To God: we locate God *within* ourSelves and Know we *are* That.

This is the New Paradigm for HU-manity: Tag we're It! Not as the false identity of the ego but as Proper Identification of ourSelves as Soul, as Spirit.

How is this New Paradigm to be accessed? Is This Paradigm just for the chosen few? The elite? Those who are deemed to have the proper "background"?

As Souls we all have the same "background": we are of the Same "Material" as the Lord, God—the Sound Current or Spirit—as the Lord, God as we are created in the Same Image, the meaning of Which has been discussed earlier.

We are recipients of the Divine Inheritance. What is Our Inheritance? All approaches to Spirit proclaim It to be Knowledge of oneSelf or True Gnosis, whether it is expressed in alchemy as the transmutation of base metals into gold, the esoteric second tree in the Garden of Eden—the Tree of Life—or in the many texts of nondualistic Gnosticism of the east and west.[2]

This Knowledge is for *all* Souls for, as we have seen, It is the Divine Architect's Plan for HU-mankind. True equity and inclusion! A True Democracy!

It is the Knowledge of oneSelf found in and with Proper Identification. But how is It found? The answer is quite simple: Initiation Into The Sound Current On The Path Of Soul Transcendence.

As we *are* One and The Same as the Lord, God, there is no "connection" to be made as there is no separation. There is just the Awakening into True Knowledge of ourSelves as The Divine Oscillation—the Lord, God.

Pure and simple!

Entrées

You ARE Soul
You ARE Spirit.
God Lives In You As You.

We have Learned and digested much from the Appetizers. We have understood that the simple fact that we are "created in God's Image" means that we are Created out of the Holy Spirit, out of the Sound Current.

We also know that God—the Divine Oscillation—is the Great Oversoul and because we are of the Same "Material"—however nonmaterial—we *are* Soul, we *are* Spirit.

We have also discovered the meaning of "In my Father's house are many mansions" so we know that there are many Levels or Realms—also called Frequencies—in Spirit and we have also uncovered a Great Secret and That is that the Location of "the Father's House with many mansions" is *within*.

As we know That we *are* Soul and That This Soul lives *within* us and that This Soul is comprised of all the Levels or Frequencies of Spirit, including That of the Great Spirit or God, then it is self-evident that God lives *within* us in the Housing we call "the body".

We can only conclude that the simple fact is that GOD LIVES IN US AS US is the Truth.

. . . .

We are called human beings. We are called to be HU-man.

As discussed, HU is The First Manifestation of the Lord, God, the Great Spirit or Oversoul. That tells us What we *are*: Manifestations of the Lord, God. As we can only Manifest What we *are*, it stands to reason that we *are* Spirit, that God lives in us as us.

HU, as we have discovered, sits at the "top" of the Spiritual Heavens, which is only logical as It is The Divine Oscillation's First Manifestation. As such, It has "Dominion" over all. Not in the sense of power and control but, rather, in terms of "above"—having a Higher Frequency—than all the Other Frequencies or Realms.

We, as HU-man Beings, have This Responsibility. We are HU-man Beings called forth to be HU-man Beings by Progressing through all the Levels or Realms—the Frequencies—up to, and including, the HU Oscillation.

This Responsibility—the Ability to Respond as the Spirit we *are*—to Know That we *are* God in Manifestation, That God lives in us as us by being able to Hold and Maintain the HU Frequency, is now available to the whole of HU-mankind *while in the body*.

. . . .

This "jump" from Souls being in "limboland" to Souls being able to Enter What's called Eternal Life by Knowing Themselves—an Inner, Initiatory Process through Initiation

Into The Sound Current or Holy Spirit and following *exactly* The Teacher's Instructions—as Soul and Spirit, Which Completes Their Karmic Journeys on this planet and enables the Soul to continue Its Spiritual Progression through the "many mansions in My Father's House" in the Inner Worlds to the Soul's being able to do Its Entire Progression *while in the body* has just now become available because of What I call THE GRAND EXPERIMENT.

Although Souls reincarnate from different Levels or Realms "below" That of the Soul Realm, "below" That of Eternal Life, it is important to note that *all* Souls have This New Opportunity. True diversity, equality and equity!

. . . .

What is THE GRAND EXPERIMENT? Quite simply put, It involves the future evolution of the HU-man race. In the course of Souls' having the Experience Of Creation and, in the Exercising Free Will That Souls were Given, They chose away from the Spirit out of Which They were Created and created thoughts and feelings away from the Lord, God. This result—karma, the separation from the Spirit Souls *are* —turned the embodiment Given to Souls to Experience the Creator's Creation into reincarnational patterns with this and subsequent exercising of Free Will into creations other than as Soul, as Spirit.

Souls had separated Themselves from Their Divine Origin and needed to reclaim Their True Inheritance. There was no way for most Souls to re-Enter into Eternal Life and "limboland" was where Souls lingered between incarnations.

Enter The Christ, Jesus. We must remember to regard the Christ as a Consciousness of God rather than as a religious figure or as the "founder" of one to understand fully the Demonstration of how to Return Home, an Opportunity Given to HU-mankind to determine whether it would be able to rise above "limboland".

We need to enter into time and space—the physical world—symbolized by the Cross and enter into the Soul Body and be with God in a Process called the Resurrection. It is not the *physical* resurrection of the dead as believed in by many ancient religions and cultures as well as current ones but the Spiritual Resurrection of the Soul Returning to God.

After the passing of this body that had anchored the Christed Consciousness, This Consciousness was passed to all Souls and this test started.

Within approximately two millennia, it was determined that HU-mankind had passed the test as enough Souls had been able to go beyond "limboland" to Return To Their True Home through the Initiatory Process Of The Sound Current to begin Part Two of THE GRAND EXPERIMENT.

What is Part II of This Experiment? It is important to recall the true meaning of "In My Father's House are many mansions": that there are many Levels or Realms or Frequencies and that there are many Levels (twenty-seven) "between" the Soul Realm or Eternal Life—Where the Soul has the Ability to Hold the Frequency That enables It to sit in Perpetual Adoration[1] of the Lord, God—and the HU Realm, The First Manifestation of the Lord, God.

Souls are now being Given the Opportunity to Progress through These Realms *while in the body,* as This HU Frequency has entered the earth plane, carried by the Consciousness anchored in a body on this planet.

This is also why the Christ Consciousness Promised to return. It is to deliver This Part of Consciousness: Part II of THE GRAND EXPERIMENT.

• • • • • • • • • • • • •

The Inner Worlds of Spirit below the Soul Realm—the Frequency or Level That is often referred to Spiritually as Eternal Life—distinct from religious terminology are known as the psycho-material worlds. These are Levels of density.

As we work our way upwards in terms of the Frequency becoming higher these Levels become less dense. As we Progress through the Levels—the Astral; the Causal—where the emotions sit as do the karmic records—; the Mental and the Etheric, the Mental is less dense than the Causal, for example, and is denser than the Etheric One.

As noted, Souls have karma on These Levels—albeit in different variations and proportions from each "Other"—and Souls incarnate from These Levels. So, while the Earth may be labeled a "classroom" It is a classroom composed of many Spiritual Grades and, within each grade, a very large number of "projects"—fate karmas—are being worked.

Part I of THE GRAND EXPERIMENT of The Christ, Jesus consists of Souls—in however many incarnations it takes to Complete Their karmic journeys here through the Initiatory Process Of The Sound Current (or the Holy Spirit or the Word as It is called in the West) and to go Home to God, Entering Eternal Life, having Strengthened Itself by Knowing Itself and, in This Process, the karmic pulls into These Levels or Frequencies no longer influence It. The Soul has then truly "overcome the world"—and completed Its reincarnational pattern.

These psycho-material worlds are also called the dual worlds. When the Sound Current Emanating from the Lord, God enters these dual worlds It splits into the "negative" and "positive" polarities—not "good" or "bad" but as in the polarities found in batteries, for example. Along the "negative" polarity the Sound Current is Known as the

Light; along the "positive" polarity It is Known as the Sound.

The Spiritual Light can travel along both polarities but the magnetic light—that which emanates from Levels in the dual worlds—can only travel along the "negative" pole. That is why, when a person says that they "work with the Light", it is important to ask from where It originates to determine whether It is the magnetic Light or the Spiritual Light as you may wish the Latter to be your Choice.

Above these dual worlds—the importance of the bipolar worlds can never be overstated as they give the Initiated Soul the Opportunity to Choose into Spirit on These Levels, into the Positive Polarity, rather than be fated to live along the negative polarity in "negativity"—sits the Unipolar Existence of Spirit.

As noted, there are Twenty-Seven Additional Levels above the Soul Realm That Part II of THE GRAND EXPERIMENT is now making available to all Souls *while in the body*. This, with very rare exceptions, was not available before.

Each of these Twenty-Seven Levels or Frequencies or Divine Oscillations sits *within* the Soul Present with each of us. As we, according to God's Pleasure, were created to Know ourSelves as Souls—being the Same as The Oversoul—in This Process we Know and Love God and Fulfill the Purpose Of Our Creation As Soul.

Our Journey as Soul is One of a Traveler. It is not, however, that we travel from Point A to Point B. In the lower worlds, the dual worlds of density, the Initiated Soul—by following the Spiritual Instructions *exactly* as Imparted At The Time Of Initiation—rises in the Frequency It can hold by Focusing on the Upper Part Of The Third Eye and, thus, through these karmic sheaths around the Soul a Path is Cleared and the Consciousness is Present with the Soul on the Level to Which

This Path has been cleared. The Level was always Present but, because of creations away from Spirit—the karma—the Consciousness was separated from the Soul but is now in the Process of Returning to Soul Consciousness or Eternal Life, also called the Christed Consciousness.

Once the Soul has Entered into Eternal Life, It continues on Its Journey. It now engages in a Two-fold Process: on one hand, It continues Its Upvibration Pattern, continuing to be able to Hold Higher and Higher Frequencies of the Levels above the Soul Realm as It continues to sit in Adoration of the Lord, God and, on the other hand, now that It has the Spiritual Strength to do so, It clears the karma left behind[2] while The Teacher stands aside supervising as a "Big Brother" rather than the Initiated Soul's Following The Teacher in the Inner Worlds as was true before the Soul was able to Hold These Frequencies.

The Soul's Awakening above the Soul Realm to all These Realms or Divine Oscillations and being Fully Conscious of Them is referred to as the Spiritual Traveler Consciousness.

It is important to once again note that This Consciousness is in *every* Soul.

It is also extremely important to note that, like all Spiritual Actions, this One is always true: we are Given only that which we as Souls can handle.

And we have been Given this New Dispensation That is Our Responsibility as HU-man Beings to Fulfill. We, indeed, have the Ability to Respond as the Spirit we *are*.

Simple.

Your Will And God's Will Are One And The Same

"In the Beginning was the Word and the Word was with God." As we have discovered earlier, the Word is another name for the Holy Spirit or for the Sound Current. We have also Learned that, despite its seemingly very real appearance, the separation between humans and the Divine Oscillation —the Lord, God—is an illusion caused by the karma that has been created during the Soul's many reincarnations that separates It from Itself.

It is often bantered about that "we are all One". Many human beings have asserted this in what is called their or humanity's "finest moments"—from philosophers and religious leaders to world leaders to brilliant scientists like Tesla and Einstein.

But how many have asserted the Simple Truth of humanity's Oneness with God? We have been told that the Christed Consciousness in Manifestation is The Same as the Lord, God.

As we have Learned, the Christed Consciousness is Our Will and God's Will are One and The Same. Let us look at What "God's Will" means!

God's Will—simply stated—is to Exercise Our Free Will to Choose into Knowing God. Just as the Lord, God created us as Souls out of the Same "Material"—the Holy Spirit or Sound Current That The Great Oversoul is—to Experience all of the Divine's Creation so, too, are we to Know ourSelves as Soul, as Spirit as Knowing ourSelves as Soul, as Spirit *is* Knowing God as It is all One.

As we have previously discovered, Souls Exercised Their Free Will to choose into the world of form that They were experiencing and, thus, created separation or karma: a reflection of Their Choice and of Their Power to Create.

Because of this Souls were "in a pickle". Having chosen into false ID—into identifying with thoughts and feelings—rather than into Their Proper ID as Souls, Souls had fallen away from Themselves rather than Knowing Themselves as Soul, as Spirit.

How can Souls That have Exercised Their Free Will to choose into other than God's Will and the resulting illusion of separation from The Divine Oversoul be in Alignment with God's?

Simple! The very Gift That was used to be in false ID is to be used to be in Proper ID as Soul: the Exercising of Free Will.

Humans as Soul, as Spirit can Exercise Their Free Will to Choose into the Spirit They *are*.

How is this possible? For Souls not Initiated Into The Sound Current when negativity comes up—anger, fear, hurt, etc.—Choose to drop it by using any of The Tools in the Dessert Section, no matter how "gripping" or real it may seem. Then karma does not deepen and—depending upon the fate karma Present with the Soul—may complete it or no new karma is created from that particular reincarnation.

There are also many supplemental ways to do this; for example, by doing physical exercise, reading, singing and many others. What is most important is that each time this appears it is regarded as an Opportunity to Choose other than into our thoughts and feelings.

God, in His Mercy and Kindness, has Given Souls a Pathway to be in Proper ID as Souls, as Spirit and That is Initiation Into The Sound Current. An Initiated Soul has the Opportunity to be with the Spirit. It is simply by Following The Master's Instructions Given At The Time Of Initiation. An Initiated Soul—through the Office Of The Christ—has *direct access* to Spirit on the Level or Realm That It is on below the Soul Realm[1]—or What is Eternal Life—and through the It of Itself on That Realm and all the Realms—Frequencies— That are a Higher Vibration.

We have Learned that the Sound Current travels from the Lord, God through the Unipolar Existence of Spirit and when It reaches the Soul Realm splits into two below It, into "negative" and "positive" polarities and that a Soul Initiated Into The Sound Current has Exercised Its Free Choice to Know Itself as Soul, as Spirit and, thus, has *direct access* to Spirit along the Positive Polarity below the Soul Level and to the Unmediated Spirit at That Frequency and above.

As we have noted, the Choice into this false ID or Proper ID—without mitigating the conditioning that karma has placed upon it—is ours to make, as the Lord, God has Given us Free Will. Our Ability to Choose is *inherent* within Our Consciousness and can be Exercised to meet our Soul's Longing to Return Home from Whence It came and to give up our false identification with the world of form that has resulted in the bone-crushing weariness of reincarnational patterns!

Just as we as Souls were Willed into Being by The Great Oversoul—God's Will—Our Will is to be That: Soul. As we have Learned, it is Our Responsibility to be That and we have the Ability to Fulfill Our Responsibility—the Ability to Respond as Spirit—because we *are* That.

We also have discovered that the Divine Architect's Plan is that *each* Soul Returns Home and that Part I of THE GRAND EXPERIMENT is that Souls have the Wonderful Opportunity to Complete Their reincarnational patterns *while in the body* because of the Distribution of the Christed Consciousness to each Soul and to Fulfill The Master Plan for Humanity.

Because of This Distribution of Our Will and God's Will as One and The Same the Christed Consciousness is now *innate* within us as Souls. It is simply a matter of Activation.

While the Christed Consciousness is innate within us as Souls It lies dormant, asleep and must be Awakened. This is where the Awe-some Power Of Choice comes into play.

Whether we Choose To Exercise This Power or not we create our lives. The difference is the major difference between fate and destiny. When we live in the former manner everything seems to be "just happening" to us—"fated", as it were—in a haphazard and slipshod manner over which we have no control.

When we take a look we find that disease is treated in Western Cultures as if it happens to us as a random event rather than a created event for our karmic learning and an Opportunity to have the dis-ease become an ease with Our Being. It is not something from the outside that happened against us but just the opposite.

When we live in Our Destiny we have Chosen into Responsibility and into the First Cause—Spirit, The Great Oversoul, the Lord, God or Divine Oscillation, Whatever you wish to call It—rather than being at the effect of whatever the cause—the karma—that we created and that is assigned to each lifetime that is known as our fate karma.[2]

Having made That Choice, That Soul is assigned in Perfect Timing an incarnation when It meets The Master Who Gives It The Opportunity to go Home through Initiation Into The Sound Current.[3] Eventually, *every* Soul makes This Choice and the Purpose of Human Life is Fulfilled.

While it may seem like This is a "done deal" It is up to each Soul to determine when. It is in complete charge of Its Timing to end Its reincarnational pattern. You can see how Powerful we as Souls *are*.

What does This Power consist of? It is the Power Of Choice and This Power is the Power Of Surrender.

To What are we Surrendering? Is it to something outside of ourSelves? Some authority? Some god out there? A set of rules? A religion? A code of behavior?

None of the above.

We are Surrendering to the Spirit we *are*, to Our Destiny.

In short, we are simply Surrendering to ourSelves.

. . . .

We have solved the "location question". We now Know that God is located *within*. What had seemed to be a dichotomy—Spirit vs. matter, God in Heaven and humans on the Earth—was just a result of our projections. As HU-mans grew in Consciousness more and more of the Divine could be accepted until What I call the Growth of Human Consciousness has grown to Accept Its Divinity and Its Oneness.

Part I of THE GRAND EXPERIMENT—the Ability of Souls to Return Home, no longer to linger in "limboland"—celebrates This Acceptance with the Demonstration of the Crucifixion and Resurrection. This Demonstration for *all* Souls—remember the Christed Consciousness is a Consciousness Given to *all* Souls, regardless of any religious affiliation or lack thereof the bodies they are with profess!—signifies as well as Demonstrates that we have the Ability to rise above time and space—the crucifixion of our ego—and Enter Eternal Life by going into the Spirit That we *are*, into Our Consciousness That is now Christed or at One with the Lord, God.

This Demonstration is the Truth for *all* Souls and not simply a one-off Demonstration by a Master Soul.

. . . .

We now Know that God's Will is that we Know ourSelves as Soul, as Spirit, and that, when we do, we Know Our Destiny and Our Oneness with and as the Lord, God, Which is the definition of the Christed Consciousness.

It is important that we are reminded of What This Knowing is. Is it words? Belief? Feeling? Group think? A mental process? Cognition?

None of the above.

The capitalization of the "K" in Knowing gives us the answer. It is the Divine in us—the Soul—Knowing Itself. This Knowing is not of the mind, for the mind cannot enter into Spirit. It is of the Soul. How does the Soul have Its Knowing?

The Soul Learns through Its Experiences. This Experiential Learning—as the Soul Itself—is Vibrational. We Know that the Soul's Spiritual Progression begins with Initiation Into The Sound Current or Holy Spirit and is based upon the Soul's Ability to Hold the Frequency of the Realms—the "many mansions" of the Bible. This is done by Following *exactly* The Instructions At The Time Of Initiation Given By The Master, including keeping the Focus on the Godpoint. When the Soul can Hold the Frequency of the Soul Realm It is Being Itself. This Knowing *is* Being.

We were called into Being by the Lord, God: God's Will. When we Know ourSelves as Soul by Being It—able to Hold the Frequency of the Soul Realm—then Our Will and God's Will are One and The Same: to Know ourSelves as Soul.

. . . .

We also now need to take another look at What It means for the Soul to Be Itself!

With the launch of Part II of THE GRAND EXPERIMENT Souls have the Miraculous and Marvelous Opportunity to not only Enter Eternal Life Where the Soul is free from reincarnational patterns—the Gift of Part I—but also to continue Their Spiritual Progression through the Twenty-Seven Levels into the HU Level—The First Manifestation of the Lord, God—*while they are in the body*.

The Soul now has the Opportunity to Know Itself by Being Itself on all the Levels It Lives on, including HU and, thus, Complete the Spiritual Destiny of HU-mankind.

We Know from The Teachings Of The Path Of Soul Transcendence that we as Souls have This Responsibility— the Ability to Respond as the Spirit we *are*—and that Part II of THE GRAND EXPERIMENT is the verification of This Fact.

There Is No "Death"

Our notion of "death" is made understandable by the illusion of separation perpetuated by unworthiness.

We have Learned much about how this illusion of separation is created and that we are responsible for doing so. The mind, which wishes to remain in charge and will do anything to maintain its position, creates the illusion that we are simply isolated beings on this planet and forces us to believe that we are living in a three-story building when, in fact, we are living in a ten-story one.

But our mind does not have the power to maintain its hegemony unless we give it this power.

How do we give the mind this power? As we have discussed, we have been Given Free Will to Choose and we have Exercised It and used It to make choices away from the Spirit we *are*. This karma that we have created and for which we *are* Responsible obscures all the other floors in our ten-story building to such an extent that we do not know that there are additional floors.

With the mind in charge we can only live in the world of opposites—of yin and yang—with categories that help us "understand" and with labels that make it seem as if we do.

We have also Learned that the mind is "hooked up" with what are called basic selves that bring forth our karma for this lifetime—known as our fate karma—whose only job is to ensure that we return and return and return to this planet in a seemingly never-ending reincarnational pattern.

We also know that this sense of being isolated beings adrift on this planet—no matter how hard we may work to cover this up—leads us to seek to build monuments to ourSelves so that we leave a record of ourSelves of having been here.

These monuments may be of fame, money, status or other physical ones but they all reflect the basic sense that we are unknown to God and have been cast adrift.

This karma creates the illusion of separation that, in turn, reinforces it in a vicious cycle. Our improper identification with our thoughts and feelings—the means by which karma is created—leads to the seeming conclusion that, once our thoughts and feelings cease when the body is no more, "death" exists as our identity is no more.

Parallel with the above is the phenomenon—demonstrated by Adam and Eve in the Garden of Eden—that runs through people: unworthiness. Adam and Eve covered up their nakedness—their not wearing the "clothing" of the Lower Frequencies or Realms in the dual worlds, those sheaths around the Soul, and were in the Soul Body—because they felt ashamed. They felt shame because they felt that they could not "measure up" to the Spirit That they *are*.

But there is a second tree in the Garden of Eden: the Tree of Knowledge of Good and Evil. This Tree symbolizes that we—as people like Adam and Eve—have a Choice and Our

Choice is to serve God or the things of the world. In other words, to have Proper ID or live in improper identity. And that we have a Purpose here.

If we take a closer look at this Tree we will notice a very important "fruit" of this exploration. It tells us the true purpose of the mind. Rather than be in charge and, in the process, create the illusion of a ten-story building having only three floors its purpose is to serve God.

But how can the mind serve God and allow Our Consciousness to Know that That Which it serves *is* the Spirit That Our Consciousness *is* when we feel unworthy?

We need to recognize that this feeling is just that—a feeling—and that it serves as a protective mechanism. What is being protected but the hegemony of the mind and our identification with a feeling, which is the very definition of improper identification and the cause of our reincarnations that we have created and perpetuates the illusion of separation.

We have Learned that we are created in God's Image, that we are of the Same "Material"—known as the Sound Current, or Audible Life Stream or Holy Spirit in the West and as Shabd in the East—as God, The Great Spirit. If God has made us from Himself, as it were, then God has found us worthy. That is why The Teachings That I Bring Forth Of The Path Of Soul Transcendence Teach That we are *Inherently* Worthy. Our Worthiness exists *a priori*. We do, indeed, "measure up" and the shame that was experienced in the Garden of Eden—the feeling that we do not "measure up" to God—is exposed for what it is: an illusion.

This event in the Garden of Eden is a mirror image of what we have done in Our Consciousness: we have kicked God out, expelled Him, as it were, and we keep doing this and doing this by creating away from the Spirit we *are*, separating ourSelves further and further from ourSelves as Spirit, expelling ourSelves more and more from Our Consciousness.

We Know that Our Consciousness is a Christed Consciousness regardless of the religion or lack thereof that the body the Soul is with professes as It simply means Our Will and God's Will are One and The Same and that people of all religions and faiths have exemplified This Consciousness.

Our Will That is One and The Same with God's serves as the dispeller of this illusion of separation and as the Divine's "motor" throughout our many incarnations to re-unite with the Spirit we *are*—Our True and Only Soulmate.

God in His Kindness and Mercy has provided a Way— Initiation Into The Sound Current to complete our karmic journeys on this planet—the only Realm or Level for Souls to do This in the negative or dual worlds—thanks to Part I of THE GRAND EXPERIMENT.

What does the Successful Completion of Part I that has enabled Part II of THE GRAND EXPERIMENT to be launched have to do with the Truth That "death" does not exist?

Everything.

The "death" of a HU-man Being simply means the cessation of life in this form. We Know that What animates the body is the Soul, That Which is made of the Same "Material" as The Great Oversoul or the Lord, God.

We also Know that once the Soul leaves the body that within an hour or less the body is considered "dead".

But there is also another definition of "death" that deals with the Spiritual Reality of the HU-man race as Souls in physical bodies.

The tale of the phoenix rising out of the ashes of the old self with renewed youth tells us of This Reality of HU-man Beings coming into the world and "dying" and from this "death"—the phoenix is burned on its funeral pyre—rising anew.

What are the ashes but our bodily form. What rises from this form but the Soul. This not only depicts the Reality of the nonexistence of "death" but also Our Purpose here: to come into bodily form so we can Rise or be Resurrected.

What is being Resurrected? Is it our bodies? Our minds? Our feelings? We have Learned that, unlike the many interpretations of various religions and beliefs, and their practices that it is not the physical resurrection of the dead. We know that What is rising from the body is the Soul, not the body itself.

We also know that once a Soul has left the body It returns to the Inner Worlds at the same Frequency It Vibrated at while It was in the body and is subject to karma and reincarnation[1] because of the karma—the choices away from the Spirit It *is*—It had created in that and previous incarnations. The Soul continues Its existence even though the body is no more.

The Soul subject to karma and reincarnation and living in the Lower Realms below the Soul Level or Realm is still involved with "death" and its illusion as It takes on body after body in bodies that lose their aliveness—their animation— when the Soul leaves it.

Part I of THE GRAND EXPERIMENT gave Souls the Opportunity to Enter into the Soul Realm, into Eternal Life Where It is no longer subject to reincarnation patterns and into Which *every* Soul will enter according to the Divine Blueprint and Initiation Into The Sound Current or Holy Spirit or Holy Shabd was and is the means to do so.

The Resurrection is not of the physical body but of the Soul Body.

Underneath It All Is Love

"God's Love for His Children" is a phrase we hear bantered about in places of worship and in comments about the state of the world. The phrase is commonly discussed as one in which we are outside of the parameters—we have sinned; we are unworthy; we have been expelled, for example—and no longer qualify to be a Child of God and/or we begin an evidentiary proceeding using the state of the world to refute the Truth that God Loves us.

We have a sense that "God is Love" takes place in the sky, in the heavenly sphere but does not apply in the kingdom we live in called the Earth. God is removed from this world and only people on the fringes of the world and their minds and groups reflecting this would even act as if "God is Love" was true. Even those who profess belief lean towards it as an ideal—something out of reach—and struggle with how to bring it into reality.

Can it be brought into this world by following rules laid down by religion? Can it be activated by some magic formula if it exists at all? If it is true is my attempt to live it doomed to failure? What do I need to do?

. . . .

Practicing Proper Identification, we Know That we *are* Soul. We Know that we are Given as many Opportunities—called lifetimes—as we need to come into the *Conscious* Knowing of ourSelves as Soul.

These Opportunities are like a parent's teaching their child for as long as it takes for the child to get the learning after the lesson has been demonstrated. Patience, neutrality—no judgements—and encouragement reflecting the knowing that the child will eventually master the lesson are all part and parcel of the unconditional loving of the parent.

The Great Oversoul—the Divine Oscillation—Holds His Creation in Love and in Loving.

We have Learned that the Divine Blueprint is that *all* Souls Complete their karmic journeys and go Home to God. So the KNOWING is there. But we were not left alone to figure out how.

God's Love is *active*; It is the Loving. God's Loving put the Knowing That we will *all* Return Home by Knowing ourSelves as Souls into the Divine Blueprint carried by The Christ. One of the Holders of This Spiritual Office was the One known as The Christ, Jesus. He Demonstrated That we need to give up our identities as egos—identified with time and space, which is death—and be in the Resurrected Body—the Soul Body—and be with God. After The Christ, Jesus left the body the Christed Consciousness was Distributed to *all* Souls.

We are shown What Our True Purpose *is*. It wasn't hidden; it wasn't abstracted or obscured. Because of our collective karma we may not have understood It just as a child may not understand a parent's love when it does, in fact, exist.

We have also Learned that in order for a Soul to Complete Its karmic journeys and Return Home to the Lord, God It needs to be able to Hold the Frequency of the Soul Realm and we Know that Souls can only Vibrate in the Inner Worlds at the same Frequency at which It could *while in the body* so that there needs to be the Opportunity *while in the body* to Vibrate at the Frequency of the Soul Realm.

We know that Part I of THE GRAND EXPERIMENT Gave Souls This Opportunity. Souls confined to "limboland" could now Progress to the Soul Realm *while in the body* and Enter Eternal Life. It is God's Love turned into Action—LOVING—that gave Souls This Opportunity.

God not only Gave Souls the Opportunity but also, because we as Souls were created from the Same "Material", Gave Souls The Gift of Himself called the Sound Current, the Shabd, the Holy Spirit, the Audible Life Stream. While Known by many Names, It provides The Method.

Regardless of by What Name It is called, The Method[1] is the same: Initiation of the Soul Into This—the Sound Current —and the Following *exactly* of The Teacher's Instructions Given At The Time Of Initiation.

While This Method has been here for thousands of years, with the Gift of Part I of THE GRAND EXPERIMENT Souls were now able to Enter into Eternal Life, free from the cycle of karma and reincarnation. This is the meaning of the phrase that The Christ, Jesus came and "conquered death".

This conquering of "death" is not based upon beliefs or non-belief, following precepts or understanding concepts. The

Soul That is to be Initiated Into The Sound Current on This Inner Path is Given the Names of God That are Spiritually Charged by The Master That enable the Soul to Progress through the Realms.

The Teachings That I Share are known as a *Bhakti* Path. This Path is a Devotional One, Centered in Love and in Loving. The Initiate, as They Grow in Love by Progressing Spiritually by daily *Simran* and *Dhyan* through the Inner Worlds, Grows in Love for The Teacher, and thus, for the Lord, God.

As God can be an amorphous, vague "concept" to a Being in a body The Teacher is the focal point for God in this world of form. God needs to be represented in a physical form so that a Soul in a physical body can relate to It.

It is important to note—especially to Westerners—that The Teacher is not the physical form of the body of That Teacher. The True Teacher is the Spiritual Form of The Teacher That is One With And As the Lord, God. This Soul has already Completed Its Spiritual Journey and, no longer Individualized, has Merged back into the Body of God. God —in His Love and Compassion and Knowing the importance of the need to take on form for Beings in the physical world— Dispatches Himself, as it were.

The Master then can only be truly related to from the Spirit we *are*. Improperly identifying ourSelves as the body we are occupying with its thoughts and feelings leads to the improper viewpoint of seeing The Teacher as "outside" of us and allows the ego's construct of power and control to rule in the relationship between Initiate and Teacher.

Nothing can be further from the Truth. It is God's Love That, Through God's Will in action by entering the world of form, is Loving—the very basis of This Path and of the relationship of Initiate and Teacher and That *is* the Lord, God Himself.

A Student on The Path Of Soul Transcendence *is* a Lover of God. Not ideas about God; not beliefs; not representations of God nor any theology but the Soul's Inner Experience Of Itself as Soul, as Spirit as, in fact, the Living God. That is the Knowing of Itself as Soul, as Spirit as the Living God Realized by Following *exactly* the Spiritual Instructions Given At The Time Of Initiation.

. . . .

We have come to Learn that Part II of THE GRAND EXPERIMENT is in place now and that Souls can now, once Established in the Soul Realm—also known as Eternal Life—Progress through the many Realms or Frequencies "above" It up to, and including, the HU Realm—The First Manifestation of God—*while in the body.*

This is the reason the Path is Named The Path Of Soul Transcendence. The Soul can Rise above the Level of Being Home in the Soul Realm and can Transcend Itself—Know more of Itself—*while in the body.* Wow!

. . . .

We have discovered that we as Souls were Created for God's Purpose to Know the Creator and His Creation. Having been endowed with Free Will, we as Souls Exercised It to create choices other than God and, by doing so, established reincarnational patterns for ourSelves and began to live in the illusions of the karmic fields that resulted.

God gives us the Gift of Himself—the Sound Current or Holy Spirit or Holy Shabd—as a Ladder for us to climb out of these karmic fields of our making.

Then to help Souls further in Their Progression, in the vastness of "time" and its illusion, God sends the Demonstrator of the Consciousness of the Oneness of God and HU-manity to Demonstrate the Process of Returning Home to Our Original State of Being One with God and then re-Ignites Our Consciousness to do so—to be able to Progress from "limboland" to Our Eternal Home.

The Gift of God Creating us as Souls to Know Him and His Creation; God's Knowing of Our Ability to Exercise Our Responsibility—Our Ability to Respond as the Spirit we *are*—includes Our Ability to Know ourSelves as Spirit on *all* Levels up to, and including, HU and so God has now made Available to us as Souls in bodies all These Realms That had previously, with very rare exceptions, only been Accessible after the Soul had Entered Eternal Life *while in the body* and then left the body to continue Its Journey.

· · · · · · · · · · · · · ·

The Gift of Himself—the Sound Current or Holy Spirit —so that no Soul gets "lost" in Its reincarnational pattern, the Gift of the Opportunity to Return and leave "limboland" *while in the body* and the Gift of Accessing *while in the body* all the Levels of Spirit That is now available to us are all, quite simply, Gifts of Love.

For underneath it all—under all the karmic fields that we have created by our choosing into creations other than the Spirit we *are*—and through it—the Patience and the Allowing of Our Choices and Learning—and over it is LOVE IN ACTION or LOVING.

ENTRÉE FIVE

The Work/Focus

We have Learned/discovered that the Divine Blueprint has been drafted—drawn—and implanted into each and every Soul and that the Divine Architect's Plan—THE GRAND EXPERIMENT—was Given in two stages: when The Christ, Jesus came and Demonstrated the Resurrection Process or Being in the Soul Body and rising above time and space to be with the Lord, God in Eternal Life and then passed along This Consciousness to all Souls to be done while alive in the body; thus, Giving Souls the Opportunity to be freed from "limboland" and then the Gift Given now to all Souls of the Opportunity to Progress through all the Levels or Realms in the Worlds of Spirit above the Soul Realm to the HU Realm—The First Manifestation of the Lord, God—*while in the body*.

This Divine Blueprint tells us Our Purpose and Our Responsibility to Fulfill It. It is Spirit's Plan for HU-mankind—for Itself—That is unfolded to be "read" by all Souls

and Fulfilled by all through the medium of time and space—
our sojourns as Souls on Earth through our reincarnational
patterns.

We have also come to Understand that Responsibility is
the Ability to Respond as the Spirit we *are* and That we have
This Ability because we were Given It by being Created out
of the Same "Material" as the Lord, God—the Spirit or the
Sound Current—and Nurtured by Spirit's Love to see that
It is Fulfilled by the Granting of as many Opportunities as
we need to "grow into" It, called our reincarnations. Patience
based upon Knowing of Our Fulfillment of This: True Love!

We Exercise This Ability by Exercising the Gift we were
Given as Souls when we were first created: Free Will. While
it may seem paradoxical to say we have Free Will and that the
Choice will be made by all Souls in the inevitable Fulfillment
of Spirit's Blueprint the Knowing That all Souls will make This
Choice does not negate Choice.

What is It That Souls are Choosing into? The Fullfillment
of Themselves as Souls, as Spirit. What is This Fulfillment?
How is It Fulfilled?

. . . .

The Soul, as we have Learned, lives on many Levels in
the Inner Worlds, some of Which are in the dual worlds also
known as the worlds of form and most of Which are in the
Pure Worlds of Spirit, Which I have dubbed the "Clear, Cold
North Country". We have discovered that the Office Of The
Christ is not affiliated with any religion but is a Spiritual Office
in charge of Souls in the dual worlds and that One of the Office
Holders was known as The Christ, Jesus Who brought in Part
One of THE GRAND EXPERIMENT—the Frequency

of the Soul Realm—and, through the Demonstration of and the Bequeathing of This Vibratory Frequency—the Christed Consciousness—to HU-manity after His leaving the body, enabled Souls to be able to Enter Eternal Life and be One with God.

We have also discovered that when Souls Enter Eternal Life They need to be able to Hold the Frequency of the Soul Realm and be able to be with the Lord, God—not subject to karma and reincarnation—and that the Soul's Progression continues in the Worlds of Spirit—the Unipolar Existence.[1] We know that HU-manity has been Gifted with Part II of the GRAND EXPERIMENT in Fulfillment of Itself as HU-manity: the Ability to Progress Spiritually through the Realms in the Worlds of Pure Spirit—Twenty-Seven Realms or Levels—to the HU plane, The First Manifestation of the Lord, God.

How is This done? Quite simply and quite well.

The body with its mind and emotions is of the dual worlds and cannot go to Spirit. Unlike the belief in the physical resurrection of the dead of many religions, both ancient and current, the Resurrection is of the Soul, of the Spirit.

This Resurrection Process does not happen simply because we as Souls have left the physical body in the process called "death"—and had professed certain beliefs. This Resurrection Process is of the Soul, of the Spirit and is, as we have Learned, Our Work here and Our Purpose while we are occupying physical bodies.

The Approach to Spirit and of Spirit is an Inner One rather than an outer one. It is important to note that This Inner Approach of the Consciousness is with all Souls in the Souls' Blueprint and is not limited to a small number of Souls as we have come to expect with any Inner or Esoteric Approach.

· · · · · · · · · · · · · ·

The "medium" through which This Blueprint is Activated is by Initiation Into The Sound Current, also known as the Holy Spirit or, simply, Shabd. This Path That I am Honored and Blessed to Bring Forth incorporates the new Opportunity That Part II of THE GRAND EXPERIMENT Brings: the Ability to Transcend, to go "above"—in terms of Frequency or Vibration—the Soul Realm until the HU Realm, Which, as we have Learned, is The First Manifestation of the Lord, God. The Initiations done on This Path are known as Initiations Into The Sound Current On The Path Of Soul Transcendence.

Remember that These Initiations are not Given to the person but to the Soul Living within. The person, after applying for Initiation On This Path and, if Approved, meeting the Pre-conditions of Preparation set by The Teacher, Which may include Attending Meditations Of The Light Of The Most High and Satsangs[2] to begin the Attunement Process and the Candidate's Presenting Themselves to The Teacher or Designated Initiator. The Candidate needs to Exercise Its Free Will and be physically Present.

The Soul within the Candidate is then "Sparked Awake" by The Master (or Designated Initiator); this "Quickening" of the Soul Stirs the dormant Soul Awake and It pulsates to Life. The Soul then Receives the Spiritually Charged Names of God, with each Name representing how God is Known on the Realms in the Lower Worlds—the worlds of duality—and how God is known in the Worlds of Spirit along with a brief explanation of the characteristics of each of These Realms. It is important to note that They are the Names of the One God and not the names of several; They are the Names of THE Lord, God. That is the *Simran* part of Initiation—the Repetition of the Spiritually Charged Sacred Names of God.

The second part of the Initiation consists of the Concentration and Focusing Technique known as *Dhyan*.

The Candidate is shown This Technique and Its correlation to Where the Soul sits in the body. It is a very specific area and not—just as is generally known—the Third Eye.

In addition to the Spiritual Instruction Given At The Time Of Initiation the Spiritual Form Of The Teacher is Placed at the Crown Chakra of the Candidate and is the Wayshower[3] and Protector of the Soul within as It Walks The Path Of Soul Transcendence.

Receiving the Sacred Gift Of Initiation also includes several Guidelines set up by The Teacher to facilitate the Soul's Walking This Path and a Study Kit through Which The Teacher also Works with The Initiate.

The Sacred Gift Of Initiation Into The Sound Current On The Path Of Soul Transcendence is the medium through Which the Divine Blueprint is Activated. It is the Initiate's Responsibility to Follow It *exactly* and to Discover the Father's House—The Many Levels of the Soul—and to Know That This House is built within and lives within you as the Living God and is you.

What a Wonder-full Journey of Discovery and how much fun it is to bathe in the Balm of the Hidden Treasure!

Our Fulfilling the Spiritual Blueprint—the Purpose of our being in bodies—is both a Choice and a Responsibility That all Souls Complete. This Blueprint is crafted from the Lord, God's LOVE and is LOVE—and Our Following The Divine Blueprint is Our Loving the Lord, God: a Wonder-full, Peaceful, yet very flesh-and-blood and Magnificent Relationship with ourSelves as Spirit.

It is What we do as Walkers On The Path Of Soul Transcendence. We are, quite simply, Lovers of God.

And in Our Walking This Path we Discover that we as Lover and the object of Our Love—the Lord, God—and the space "between" us are all One and The Same. It is all LOVE: the very Nature of Reality.

. . . .

The Focus That we have—Loving the Lord, God Who is us—is, in fact, The Path. Through This Gift Of Initiation Into The Sound Current On The Path Of Soul Transcendence we have the Opportunity to Know the Lord, God and to Know ourSelves as Soul, as Spirit, as we are One and The Same.

This is a Remembrance of Who and What we *are*. We become again What we always were: the Living God. We become again Members of the Community of Souls, this time Fully Realizing the Exercising Of Our Free Will.

To assist in This Realization Process there are several key precepts that both assist in helping us as Souls be Lovers of God and are a result of That Focus. We must re-enforce that, as Lovers of God, we are not Lovers of theology or of rituals or of any ideations about God—which we respect—but rather through direct experience enabled by Initiation Into The Sound Current On The Path Of Soul Transcendence, Which gives us the Ability to be with God on the Realm on Which we are working—the Level to Which we have Spiritually Progressed at that point.

The first important precept concerns the viewpoint of why we are on this planet. As described earlier, many of us walk around with an attitude of having been expelled from the Garden, having fallen, as it were, from Grace because we have "sinned" and that being on the Earth is our punishment. The Teachings Of The Path Of Soul Transcendence Teach us that we are here because of God's Boundless Love for us, that we have incarnated to be Given another Opportunity to Come to

Know ourSelves as Soul. While we have created away from this Knowing, God Gives us as much time and as many Opportunities—our reincarnations—as we need to come into This Knowing. It is God's Kindness and Loving That Brings us here.

Many of us also walk around with the notion that karma is "bad" and that we have come to work it off as if Earth is a work prison rather than the world being the Sacred Opportunity to "springboard"—through the Gift Of Initiation Into The Sound Current—into our Knowing and Remembrance of ourSelves as Spirit, as Soul.

The Teachings also Teach us that karma is neither "good" nor "bad" but simply Opportunities to Choose into the Spirit we *are*; that karma is separation from Our True Nature—the Divine—That is the Focus of The Teachings.

The Teachings Teach us that the only "sin" is the "sin" of not Knowing Who we *are*, the "sin" of ignorance—ignoring the Spirit we *are*. It is said that "Knowledge is Power"; It is the Knowledge of yourSelf and the Power is That of the Spirit you *are*.

Another important precept, as we have already seen, is that we are One with Spirit. In Our Consciousness sits the illusion of Spirit versus matter or a grand division between the two caused by the mind's wish to maintain control. Spirit gets projected to be "out there", in the sky, and we become, in fact, disempowered as our egos seek dominance. We are told that we have "dominion over all things". This Dominion is not over others, not of power and control, but of all of Spirit by Knowing ourSelves as Soul, as Spirit and, as such, we sit at the Apex Of Creation. The HU Realm resides within the Soul and is The First Manifestation of the Lord, God.

The ego is considered in many spiritual paths as needing to be obliterated or sidestepped or ignored, as it stands in the way of Spirit or of the individual's "enlightenment". The Teachings Of This Path Teach us that the ego has its proper place. What is the ego's proper place? The ego's proper place is in Service to the Spirit we *are*. We use the ego to direct ourSelves to Focus into the Spirit we *are*, whether it is to sit in *Simran* and *Dhyan*; to use the Many Tools we have to Attune to the Spirit we *are* or do Service from the Loving Heart, for example. It is to direct *consciously* ourSelves to ourSelves just as we *consciously* directed ourSelves to take Initiation Into The Sound Current in the first place.

Another precept concerns The Guidelines That the Initiated Soul is Given At The Time Of Initiation. It is easy to view Them as something outside of ourSelves, something "imposed" upon us and as something for which we will be "punished" if we do not follow; thus, setting up a rebellion against Them. As These Guidelines were designed by The Master to ease Our Way on This Path and for Our Protection, The Teachings Of The Path Of Soul Transcendence Teach us That the Guidelines are, in Reality, an Inner Protection and that, based upon the Knowing Of The Master, we will Progress from seeing Them as something outside ourSelves to being within—just as we will Progress from seeing The Teacher as an Outer Teacher to The Inner Teacher—and What Our Soul naturally follows rather than an outer, authoritative dictum.

As noted earlier, The Path Of Soul Transcendence is a Bhakti Path: through Love for and Devotion to The Teacher the Initiate grows in Love and Devotion to the Lord, God. It is important to note that one of the key elements on This Path—one of the key foci—is that the Outer Teacher is merely the Representation of the Inner Teacher inside each Student and that This Outer Representation eases the way to This

Knowing as the Soul Progresses. As The Teacher is Awake on all the Levels of God by being able to Hold Those Frequencies and is, in fact, God in Manifestation, the Initiate Wakes Up to the Knowing That They, too, are God in Manifestation.

Although This is a Bhakti Path, the Focus is not on The Teacher but on the Inner Experience and Knowing Themselves as Soul, as Spirit, as the Lord, God in Manifestation. The Teacher simply Facilitates This.

In This Process of Awakening to Itself the Soul Learns to live in Integrity. As The Teachings Teach us, Integrity has to do with Living in the Oneness, in the Knowing That we are all One, That each of us is a Soul and That each Soul is, in fact, the Lord, God in Manifestation regardless of the Level of Awareness.

Through the Practice of What I call "Giraffe Consciousness"—the Acceptance of all situations and encounters and all parts of our life as Spiritually Correct and for Our Learning and Growth—Neutrality develops along with the Focus upon Living in Neutrality.

The Teachings Of The Path Of Soul Transcendence serve as The Guidepost for This Progression as the Initiate checks Themselves against Them and, if need be, brings Themselves into Alignment and proceeds according to The Teachings. It is important to note that the Focus is upon one's Inner Experience Of Spirit and that That is How the Student gains the Knowledge of Themselves as Spirit and that the Outer Teachings serve merely as confirmation rather than as something upon Which to base or frame the Experience.

A Bhakti Path by Its Nature is a Surrender Path. But What is the nature of This Surrender? To What are we Surrendering? To Whom?

Surrendering is unlike that encountered in the world

where power and control rule so that if one surrenders the other one "wins" and surrender is synonymous with defeat. Surrender is simply the act of "letting go".

What are we Surrendering when we "let go"? We are Surrendering our habitual responses, our karmic patterns, our creations away from the Spirit we *are*; we are using the Divine Opportunity of Initiation Into The Sound Current On This Path to Choose into Spirit, along the Positive Polarity in the dual worlds or into Spirit Itself in the "Cold, Clear North Country" of the Unipolar Existence, depending upon Where the Student is in Their Progression. It is God in Manifestation at Whatever Level the Student is.

The Surrender is not to the Outer Teacher—Who is merely the Instrument to do so by Guiding you within and by referring you to inside yourSelf—but to the Inner One. It is not to God outside of yourSelf—God only seems to be outside because of the separation caused by the karma the individual Soul has created and the resulting projection of God outside of Itself—but to the Lord, God within. In sum, the Initiate is simply Surrendering to Themselves.

• • • • • • • • • • • • • • •

Our Work, Guided by the Foci described above, is Our Responsibility. Our Purpose here is to Fulfill Our Responsibility for we, as documented throughout this book, do have the Ability to Respond as the Spirit we *are*. The Development of This Ability is predicated on Our Knowing That we *are* Spirit—the very Purpose of Our Existence throughout Our Reincarnational Pattern.

These Opportunities are Given to us out of LOVE and from LOVE: and are the very Essence of Spirit, of the Lord, God and of us as Souls—all One and The Same.

Desserts

DESSERTS

The Desserts—The Tools Of Attunement used on The Path Of Soul Transcendence—are used to help you Attune to and Be the Spirit you *are* and to sweeten the breadth and depth of Your Understanding.

Some of The Tools are paired with specific Entrées—Teachings—and some may be paired with several; all are to be used as you wish. Whether paired or not savor Them!

Paired Desserts

+ = Please see How-To Manual in the Appendix Section
** = Available by request after attending a Meditation Of The Light Of The Most High*

With Entrée One
You ARE Soul
You ARE Spirit.
God Lives In You As You.

- *Tools For Living Free* (*TFLF*)

- Satsangs (Open Talks) +

- Meditation For Health And Well-Being

- <u>The Money Workbook</u>

- *Tools For Living Free* #12 "Taking Responsibility: Tag You're It"

- *Tools For Living Free* #13 "Taking Responsibility: Tag You're It (Part II)"

- *Tools For Living Free* #56 "The Winner Is The Spirit In You"

- Video Series *Understanding The Spirit You Are* - Part I V5 – "The Power Of Choice"

- Classes

- Podcasts

- Self-Talk +

- The Checklist Class

- Blessing The Food +

- LOVE +

With Entrée Two
Your Will And God's Will Are One And The Same

- Meditation Of The Light Of The Most High +

- Eternal Vigilance +

- Living In Grace Class

- Asking For Clarity and Guidance +

- Giraffe Consciousness +

- Highest Good +

- Open Hours +

- Blue Book *

- *Understanding the Spirit You Are* – Part II V16: "What Is The Theology Of The Path Of Soul Transcendence?"

- Everyday Evolution Class I and II

- Tithing

- Two-Part Release Technique +

- The First Law Of Spirit +

- Nintendo +

- Gratitude +

With Entrée Three
There Is No "Death"

- *Understanding The Spirit You Are* – Parts I and II
- MP3 – "What Does 'The Physical Resurrection Of The Dead' Mean?: A Participatory Satsang" (A119)
- *Tools For Living Free* #36 – "Dealing With 'Death'"
- MP3 – "'Death' And Pride: A Participatory Satsang" (A130)
- MP3 – "'Death' And Its Unveiling: A Participatory Satsang" (A210)
- Giraffe Consciousness +
- RETREATS
- Satsangs (Open Talks) +

**With Entrée Four
Underneath It All Is Love**

- Being In The Presence Of The Teacher

- *Tools For Living Free* #63 – "The Democratization Of Spirit"

- MP3 – "What Is Love?" (A80)

- *Tools For Living Free* #125 "Living In Loving Cooperation"

- Giraffe Consciousness +

- Open Hours +

- The First Law Of Spirit +

With Entrée Five
The Work/Focus

- Forgiveness Clinic

- *Tools For Living Free* #47 "Fated? Forget It!"

- Self-Talk +

- *Tools For Living Free* #90 "How Do You Approach God?"

- Giraffe Consciousness +

- *Tools For Living Free* #9 "Allowing God To Be Here For You"

- SST (Simran Service Tithing)

- *Tools For Living Free* #172 "The Real Economic Crisis"

- *Tools For Living Free* #129 "Give - Then Give Some More"

- *Understanding The Spirit You Are* - Part I V4:
  "The Twin Towers Of Acceptance And Gratitude"

- *Tools For Living Free* #18 "Living By Giving"

- Proper ID +

- Service +

- The Sunday Program +

- Acceptance Clinic

Unpaired Desserts
I = Available only to Initiates Of The Sound Current
On The Path Of Soul Transcendence.

- Being in the Physical Presence of Our Beloved Teacher

- A Baker's Dozen: *Tools For Daily Living* by The
  Teacher – in English and in Spanish

- MP3s of Our Teacher's Talks – Initiate and Public

- Videos/DVDs from the Series *Understanding The
  Spirit You Are* - Parts I and II

- Classes, Clinics and Workshops

- Initiate RETREATs

- Open RETREATs

- Class Guidelines

- Protocols

- Study Guides

- Study Kits (I)

- Speaking Tours by The Teacher

- The Home Center

- Offerings at the Home Center [and via Teleconference]:
  The Sunday Program; Meditation Of The Light Of The
  Most High; Meditation For Health And Well-Being

Unpaired Desserts cont.

- Thanksgiving Meditation Of Gratitude

- Christmas Day Meditations

- The Teachings Study Group on the second Sunday of the month

- The Sunday Program

- On the second Sunday of the Month the Program includes
  a one-hour Meditation Of The Light Of The Most High
  and a *Tools For Living Free* Reading and Discussion. The
  Sunday Program on the last Sunday of the month includes
  a two-hour Meditation Of The Light Of The Most High
  followed by a Video Showing from and Discussion of
  Understanding The Spirit You Are – Parts I and II

- The Library at the Home Center

- Regional Centers

- Videos/DVDs of Satsangs

- Offerings at Regional Centers – Meditation Of The Light
  Of The Most High, Meditation For Health
  And Well-Being

- Cosmos Tree Offerings outside of the Center

- Events for Honoring/involving The Teacher (I)

Unpaired Desserts cont.

- Monthly Satsang by The Teacher

- Baby Blessings (I)

- *SpiritCentral* - the Cosmos Tree/Center For Religion And Advanced Spiritual Studies (CRASS) Newsletter; especially, the Satsang Articles—These are terrific Tools! They are The Tools of Choice for the monthly Teachings Study Group, too!

- Epage

- *Tools For Living Free*/A Toolkit containing all the *TFLF*s

- The Picture of The Teacher

- Tithing

- Donating to Cosmos Tree or CRASS

- The Divine Walk (I)

- Attending Initiations in person (I)

- Being of Loving Service

- Inviting Souls to Our Programs/Offerings

- Blue Book *

- The Money Workbook

- Open Hour +

- Seeding

Unpaired Desserts cont.

- Checklist For Daily Living (I)
- Lovingly Co-Creating with the Lord, God/Working with the Light Of The Most High
- Calling in the Light Of The Most High +
- Blessing The Food +
- Releasing Techniques +
- Asking the Lord, God for Clarity and Guidance +
- Self-Talk +
- The Teaching of Love the Lord, God with all Your Heart and all Your Soul and all Your Might and Love Your Neighbor as yourSelf and to en-Joy the Life God Has Given you
- Practicing Individual Responsibility within a Group Focus
- Keeping Commitments
- Maintaining Proper ID/Having Spiritual Reference Points
- Keeping track of dreams
- Nighttime Travel (I)
- Living The Teachings (I)
- The Love and Growth Basket at the Home Center

Unpaired Desserts cont.

- Scholarship Jar at the Home Center

- Acceptance Jar at the Home Center

- The Master's Programs

- Reading Theses written by Graduates
  of the Master's Program

- Attending Graduation Ceremonies of the Seminary
  Division of CRASS

- WHAT'S IMPORTANT?!?! written By The Teacher,
  a Magnificent Tool and Gift Given to all Those who
  attend The Teachings Study Group

- The Cosmos Tree Web site at www.cosmostree.org
  – the Cosmos Tree site is a Power-Packed Library
  and Guide to all of The Tools you need to Lift and
  Grow! Visit the site often and use These Enlightening
  Tools daily (!): the Newsletter (including a Valuable
  Archive); *Tools For Living Free* (all of Them); a
  Schedule of All Meditations; a calendar of Events
  including the popular "Epage" that comes with the
  Newsletter; Offerings including Classes and Open

Unpaired Desserts cont.

Hours with Dr. Lane; podcasts of Dr. Lane's Talks and the Cosmos Tree blog; and by going to "shop/download" the ability to purchase/Listen to every Talk by Dr. Lane (over 300 of Them!); to purchase/give yourSelf <u>The Money Workbook</u> and <u>A Baker's Dozen: Tools For Daily Living</u> by Dr. Lane as well as DVDs of *Understanding The Spirit You Are*, all 22 Shows in this popular Video Series of Spiritual Learning with and by Dr. Lane—and to give Them as Gifts to others, too! You can also sign up to receive our *SpiritCentral* Newsletter on this site.

- The CRASS Web site at <u>www.spiritcentral.org</u> – the CRASS site educates/re-educates the visitor on The Spiritual Teacher; on Initiation Into The Sound Current; on the Path Of Soul Transcendence; on Classes and Workshops for Initiates. On-site offerings include podcasts of Dr. Lane's Talks, a Valuable CRASS blog library and the complete catalog for the CRASS Master's Programs—and more. Go There!

Unpaired Desserts cont.

- Our Monthly Podcasts – be sure to check your email by the 5th of every month for These Beautiful Satsangs—and if you're not on our email list, give yourSelf the Gift of signing up for These Talks now!!! Request to be added to the mailing list by sending your name and email address to info@cosmostree.org.

- *SpiritCentral* – Our quarterly Newsletter sent by email or regular mail to all those who sign up for It!!! Request to be added to the mailing list and receive *SpiritCentral* by sending your name and email address to info@cosmostree.org.

- *Tools For Living Free* – Our quarterly educational publication emailed to all those who sign up for Our quarterly Newsletter!!! Forward Them to friends, family, loved ones, enemies!!

- Epage – Our quarterly Calendar is emailed to all those who sign up for the Newsletter!!!

- themoneyworkbook.org

Unpaired Desserts cont.

- MNN.org – visit this Web site every Thursday at 6:30 p.m. ET to watch the Two-Part Series of Spiritual Learning *Understanding The Spirit You Are* by Dr. Roger B. Lane. This is a must!!!

- Podcasts on cosmostree.org featuring Our Teacher and lots of Learning!!

- The Cosmos Tree, Inc. *Where Potential Becomes Actuality* main Facebook Page - If you are not already on Facebook, go to www.facebook.com and sign up there on the right-hand side of the home page; once you do that, simply log onto Facebook at the top of the home page by putting in your email address and password. After that, simply put "cosmos tree" (two words) in the search box at the top of the page; a list will come up; please go down the list until you see the Cosmos Tree page that says *Where Potential Becomes Actuality* and click on that.

- The CRASS Facebook page, which you can visit by logging into Facebook (see above), then putting "Center For Religion And Advanced Spiritual Studies"

Unpaired Desserts cont.

in the search box. The listing with "Non-Profit Organization" under it and the CRASS logo is the correct page.

- Instagram – go to @cosmostreecentral and @crasscentral and share the Wealth with friends, family, colleagues, enemies!

PLEASE BE RESPECTFUL OF THE TOOLS! THEY ARE SACRED.

CONTACT US / MORE INFO.

Cosmos Tree
Center For Religion And Advanced Spiritual Studies

Telephone: (212) 828-0464   Fax: (212) 828-0419

Mailing Address: 229 East 85 St. #1347
                  New York, NY 10028

To register for Classes, Clinics, Workshops, etc. or for more information for both Initiates and Non-Initiates, please email info@cosmostree.org.

To join the Cosmos Tree mailing list and receive the quarterly Events Calendar with all information regarding upcoming Classes, Clinics, Workshops and more, please send an email to info@cosmostree.org with your name and the email address you would like added to the list. Or you may visit the Cosmos Tree website under "Contact Us" cosmostree.org/contact-us/ and fill out the Newsletter sign-up form on that page, then click "Subscribe".

To request the Precious Gift Of Initiation or to learn more email info@spiritcentral.org and include "Requesting Initiation" in the email memo with your name and contact information. A member of the Initiate Community will happily get back to you.

HOW TO PARTICIPATE

If you live within 50 miles of the Home Center please attend in person. If you live more than 50 miles from the Home Center you may join via teleconference with permission.

All dates listed include holidays.

To attend in New York City:
Please email info@cosmostree.org for location information. Please arrive 15-20 minutes before as doors close promptly at five minutes before each start time! All times are Eastern Time. *Please note: Proof of vaccination or proof of a negative COVID test within 24 hours is required to enter.*

To attend via Teleconference:
Before you are granted permission to Participate, you must read and agree to the Guidelines for Participating in an Event from outside a Center. To request a copy of the Guidelines, please email info@cosmostree.org. Once the Guidelines have been signed please send (scan or photograph) back to info@cosmostree.org. When the signed Guidelines are received the teleconference information and any other information you may need to join is sent to you.

Appendix

HOW-TO MANUAL

Satsangs (Open Talks)

The first Wednesday of every month the Founder/ Director of Cosmos Tree and Center For Religion And Advanced Spiritual Studies, Dr. Roger B. Lane, Gives a Monthly Talk (Satsang or Spiritual Instruction) at the Home Center in New York City. Talks, Which are available at our Web site www.cosmostree.org and in person and via teleconference, help you to live your life from a Spiritual Perspective. All Talks help you Learn to Focus into the Spirit you *are* and to let go of anything that stands in the way as you do That.

Please arrive 15 minutes before the start time as doors close promptly five minutes before and please do not wear any perfumes; scented oils; colognes; hair sprays; gels; fresh nail polish or remover; aftershave or other chemicals. Please refrain from alcohol or drugs—*other than your prescription medication*—24 hours before attending. These Talks are free of charge with a Suggested Donation of $5. They are held the first Wednesday of every month from 6:50 p.m. to 8 p.m. Email info@cosmostree.org for location and arrival information.

To join via teleconference you must first attend an Offering at the Home Center in New York City or at our Regional Centers. For information on attending via teleconference, email info@cosmostree.org to request permission to attend.

Self-Talk

Self-Talk involves using the energy of the basic selves— the part of Our Consciousness that brings forth our karmic patterns—in a co-operative manner for Spiritual Upliftment and Growth. For a complete understanding of basic selves and of how to best work with them it is necessary to take the Everyday Evolution 1 Class. Please see note at end of Desserts re: notification of and registration for this Class.

Blessing The Food

This is done as both a way to Upvibrate the physical food you are eating and as an Attunement to the Spirit you *are*. It is to be done with a Loving Heart by saying, "For the Highest Good, Lord, God, Bless this food with the Light Of Your Presence. Thank you!"

LOVE

LOVE is, according to The Teachings Of The Path Of Soul Transcendence, Letting go Of Volition Every time. Whenever you have an insistence or feel a "have to" in your everyday life— other than in an emergency situation—it is a good indication that the karma is upon you. Drop it! You may need to do this until the "pressure" of the karma against you is off.

Initiated Souls on The Path Of Soul Transcendence can Choose into Spirit by Chanting Their Initiatory Tones.

All Souls may also do the Two-Part Release Technique and ask for Clarity and Guidance or use any Tool to help Choose into the Spirit you *are*.

Meditations

Meditations Of The Light Of The Most High:
- Mondays 7:30 p.m. to 8:30 p.m.
- Wednesdays and Thursdays 6:10 p.m. to 7:10 p.m. - *except first Wednesday of each month.*
- The second Sunday of every month 10:30 am to 11:30 am
- The last Sunday of every month 10:30 am to 12:30 p.m.

Meditation For Health And Well-Being:
- The third Tuesday of every month at 8:45 p.m.

To Participate:
If you live within 50 miles of the Home Center please attend in person.

If joining in person please arrive 15 minutes before the start time as doors close promptly five minutes before and please do not wear any perfumes; scented oils; colognes; hair sprays; gels; fresh nail polish or remover; aftershave or other chemicals. Please refrain from alcohol or drugs—*other than your prescription medication*—24 hours before attending.

In order to Participate via teleconference, you must agree to the Guidelines, Which can be obtained by emailing info@cosmostree.org and requesting Participation. If you agree to the Guidelines, please sign and return Them by noon on the day before the Meditation you would like to attend. Please fax to 212.828.0419 or you may email Them to info@cosmostree.org.

Once received, an email will be sent to you with the call-in information. Donation information is included in the Guidelines.

If you would like to continue to Participate in future Meditations, simply send the signed Guidelines again to info@cosmostree.org, by noon on the day before the Meditation you would like to attend. You will use the same call-in information that you have received for the first Meditation you joined.

Eternal Vigilance

The Practice of always choosing in a Neutral, non-judgemental way into Growth and Upliftment. For Initiated Souls on This Path It involves Choosing into Spirit by using the many Tools available; for non-Initiated Souls using The Tools rather than being propelled into the action or word or thought by the force of karma provides fertile grounds for well-being and Growth.

Asking The Lord, God For Clarity And Guidance

You may also—after dropping your plan, your agenda—ask for Clarity and Guidance by saying, "Lord, God, send me Your Light! Please give me the Clarity and Guidance I need for (this situation)." You may also do the *Two-Part Release Technique* (see pg. 87).

Giraffe Consciousness

As a giraffe eats from the top of the tree so, too, is it important for us to feed ourSelves only the highest qualities of the Opportunity to be in the body as a HU-man Being. We are in Acceptance of all situations and people and are, thus, Neutral towards all, Knowing That we *are* Spirit and that all is Given to us for Our Learning and Upliftment.

The Highest Good

When we do anything it is best to put it into the Spiritual Light for The Highest Good. This ensures that its results are for The Highest Good of all. We do this by saying, "Lord, God, send me Your Light! I put (________) into Your Light for The Highest Good. Thank you!" AND then let go of any worry or concern or attachment to the result.

Two-Part Release Technique

Call in the Light Of The Most High by saying, "For The Highest Good, Lord, God, send me Your Light and please take (<u>what you are giving up</u>) from me!"

Then tell yourSelf, "(<u>your name</u>), it's okay to let it go!"

Initiates on This Path say, "Lord, God, send me Your Light and send This Light to My Teacher and please take (<u>what you are giving up</u>) from me!" Then do Part II as described above.

You will need to let it go as God does not violate your consciousness. You may feel energy moving or being released from you as karma is, in essence, energy.

Open Hours

A Blessed Opportunity for personal Growth via an approximately 12-minute private session with Founder/Director Roger B. Lane, Ph.D. A Golden Opportunity to ask for the help you need in your life and to Learn how to live that life from a Spiritual Perspective, Which means Joyously and Peacefully by Focusing into the Spirit you *are*. Sessions Focus on Upliftment and Growth.

If you would like to call in for Open Hour you need a reservation. Go to cosmostree.org > Offerings > Open Hours and click on the calendar date that you wish to reserve; fill out the contact form and choose the first available time. Once a reservation has been made you are responsible for calling the appropriate number at the exact time and date you have chosen. There is a Suggested Donation of $15.

By telephone only.
- Tuesday 7:30 p.m. to 8:30 p.m. (ET)
- Wednesday 4:30 p.m. to 5:30 p.m. (ET)

Service

This is One of The Cornerstones Of The Teachings Of The Path Of Soul Transcendence. Because we are all One, when we Serve "others" we are really Serving ourSelves. It is a Wonderful Opportunity to be in the Spirit we *are* while assisting "other" Souls. We do so by first Centering ourSelves in and as Spirit by saying, "Lord, God, I put This Service of (Service you are doing) into Your Light for The Highest Good" and letting go into This.

It is important to Know That any Service is equally as important as any other. What is important is to be in the Loving Heart, the very Nature of the Lord, God.

Nintendo

This is a term I borrowed from the Japanese to mean to work hard and leave the results to God. If we are doing to get results—financial, emotional or otherwise—we are outside of ourSelves and, thus, creating karmically. We need to be Neutral about what we are doing and by putting it into the Light for The Highest Good (see pg. 87). We do This by being Present with it. Outcomes are not our concern.

Gratitude

Appreciation of what we *already* have been Given and the Knowing that *all* comes from the Lord, God. When Present in Gratitude lack and limitation are nonexistent.

Proper Identity (ID)

Knowing That we *are* Soul, *are* Spirit. We identify ourSelves as Soul, as Spirit and Know that the body is Its Container and that our thoughts and feelings are fleeting and not What we *are* and we are without attachment to Them.

The Sunday Program

The Sunday Program is held the Second Sunday and Last Sunday of Every Month at the Home Center.

The Program on the Second Sunday consists of the Meditation Of The Light Of The Most High and *Tools For Living Free* Reading and Discussion

- **Meditation Of The Light Of The Most High –** 10:30 a.m. to 11:30 a.m.

- *Tools For Living Free* **Reading and Discussion** – noon to 1 p.m. – a life-altering Opportunity to Grow and Strengthen yourSelf Spiritually using the educational publication *Tools For Living Free* as the Program Tool. Please READ the *TFLF* prior to attending. All *TFLF* Titles can be found at cosmostree.org under Resources.

You are encouraged to attend both parts of the Program but may attend an individual Offering as well.

There is a Suggested Donation of $5 for both parts of the Offering.

Available in person at the Cosmos Tree Home Center in New York City and via teleconference for Participants living beyond a 50-mile radius of the Home Center. If attending in person, please arrive 15 minutes before the start time as doors close promptly five minutes before and please do not wear any perfumes; scented oils; colognes; hair sprays; gels; fresh nail polish or remover; aftershave or other chemicals. Please refrain from alcohol or drugs—*other than your prescription medication*—24 hours before attending.

For those wishing to Participate via teleconference – email info@cosmostree.org by 5 p.m. the day before to request permission to attend via teleconference.

The Program on the Last Sunday consists of the Meditation Of The Light Of The Most High and the Video Showing and Discussion.

- **Meditation Of The Light Of The Most High** – 10:30 a.m. to 12:30 p.m.

- **Video Showing and Discussion** – 1 p.m. to 2 p.m. – A Discussion based on viewing a Video from the Series *Understanding The Spirit You Are* by Cosmos Tree Founder/Director Dr. Lane.

There is a Suggested Donation of $5 for both the Meditation and Video Showing.

Available in person at the Cosmos Tree Home Center in New York City and via teleconference for Participants living beyond a 50-mile radius of the Home Center. If attending in person, please arrive 15 minutes before the start time as doors close promptly five minutes before and please do not wear any perfumes; scented oils; colognes; hair sprays; gels; fresh nail polish or remover; aftershave or other chemicals. Please refrain from alcohol or drugs—*other than your prescription medication*—24 hours before attending.

For those wishing to Participate via teleconference – email info@cosmostree.org by 5 p.m. the day before to request permission to attend. Please be available to watch the Video from 1 p.m. to 1:30 p.m. from a computer or tablet before teleconferencing in.

The Teachings Study Group

A life-altering Opportunity to grow Spiritually through the Summaries of Monthly Talks offered in each issue of the Cosmos Tree/CRASS Newsletter. The Teachings Study Group is held the second Sunday of each month from 3 p.m. to 4 p.m.

Please read the Article prior to attending. All *SpiritCentral* Newsletter Articles can be found at cosmostree.org under Newsletter.

There is a Suggested Donation of $5.

Available in person at the Cosmos Tree Home Center in New York City and via teleconference for Participants living beyond a 50-mile radius of the Home Center. If attending in person, please arrive 15 minutes before the start time as doors close promptly five minutes before and please do not wear any perfumes; scented oils; colognes; hair sprays; gels; fresh nail polish or remover; aftershave or other chemicals. Please refrain from alcohol or drugs—*other than your prescription medication*—24 hours before attending.

For those wishing to Participate via teleconference – email <u>info@cosmostree.org</u> by 5 p.m. the day before to request permission to attend via teleconference.

ENDNOTES

FIRST COURSE
APPETIZER ONE

1   I have chosen to describe This Reality using the following terms because it may be more readily understandable to Western readers rather than the Indian description with terms such as *pind*, *anda*, *brahmanda*, and *parbrahm*, for example. For a further understanding of the Indian description of the Spiritual (Inner) Worlds you may wish to read Chapter 4 of The Path Of the Masters by Julian Johnson (Punjab, India: Radha Soami Satsang Beas, 1939).

The Lower Worlds consist of Levels or Realms of different Frequencies and densities and correspondences. They are noted sequentially but, in Reality, They are interpenetrating. They are the Astral Realm, Which corresponds to the imagination; the Causal Realm, to the emotions and to Where the akashic records are stored; then the Mental Realm, Where Thoughts are stored and the Etheric Realm, Which corresponds to the collective unconscious. This is "followed" by the Soul Realm or What is called Eternal Life.

2   The Bible references this in many of Its Books, whether Corinthians or Psalms, for example, as have many writers and scholars such as William Blake and Marshall McLuhan.

APPETIZER TWO

1   A discussion of the various origins of religion is found in the introduction of <u>World Religions: From Ancient History to the Present</u> edited by Geoffrey Parrinder (New York: Facts On File, 1985) 9-21.

2   This definition was brought to my attention—for which I am deeply appreciative—in conversations with Ronald Grant, D.Min., M.D., who also helped bring My Knowing about the practices at the Sacred Cave to the forefront of My Consciousness.

3   I have chosen to use the words *incarnate, incarnates* or *incarnation* to denote the Soul's Pattern of taking on a body and returning to Earth to distinguish it from embody, which is the Soul's originally lodging in a body to explore this part of God's Creation in accordance with God's Will and before Souls used Their Free Will to choose other than into the Lord, God.

4   This part of ourSelves is called the basic self. I have borrowed this term originally from Huna—a Hawaiian philosophy—to explain the energies I was experiencing directly. Basics may be male or female—negatively or positively charged as a battery is—and, before incarnating, are assigned to the Soul from a "repository" of basics according to the Soul's fate karma for that particular incarnation. Most people have two or three basics. The Everyday Evolution 1 Class is an excellent way to get a deeper understanding of them; their purpose and how to direct them.

5   The Word is another term for the Sound Current or Holy Spirit or Shabd. The quote is from John 1:1 of the New Testament. It is important to note that The Christ, Jesus states

that "he that hath seen me hath seen the Father" (John 14:9), making it very clear that the Christed Consciousness is One and The Same as the Lord, God. This confirms Our Inner Knowing That we *are* the Living God as This Consciousness was Distributed to *each* Soul when The Christ, Jesus left the body and portends both Part I and Part II of THE GRAND EXPERIMENT.

APPETIZER THREE

1   This Law of Spirit was brought to My Attention by J.R. Hinkins, DSS, who served as My Spiritual Teacher years ago and for Whose Teachings I am deeply grateful. These Teachings served as outer reference points to My Inner Experience and to Where I was in My Growth of Consciousness and Some thus are incorporated here, such as that we are only Given what we can handle; the Christ as a Spiritual Office; the Distribution of the Christed Consciousness after the "death" of The Officeholder known as Jesus; Eternally Traveling Consciousness and basic selves.

2   While none has been quoted, for further reading and understanding you may wish to read <u>The Dead Sea Scrolls</u> edited by G. Vermes (Great Britian: Penguin Books, Ltd, 1985), a translation of Those of the Qumram Community, an Essence Sect of which The Christ, Jesus was a member. You may also wish to read the four Gnostic Gospels called the Secret Book of James; the Gospel of Thomas; the Book of Thomas and the Secret Book of John. You may also wish to read the texts of Those found at Nag Hammadi and are included in <u>The Nag Hammadi Library</u> edited by James Robinson (New York: Harper and Row, 1978), which is an excellent collection of the tractates of Coptic Gnosticism.

ENTRÉES
ENTRÉE ONE

1 The Soul, once It has been Established in the Soul Realm, sits in Perpetual Adoration of the Lord, God as It can Hold the Frequency or Vibration of the Soul Realm as It has Moved into the Realization of Itself as Soul *and* is involved in two Spiritual Actions in the Inner Worlds. One is That the Soul Continues Its Progression—in a Process dubbed "Eternally Traveling Consciousness" or "ETC Consciousness"—through The Twenty-Seven Levels to HU and, also, because It now has the Spiritual Strength or "muscle" to do so, clears up the karma It has left behind in the lower worlds as The Teacher now stands by in support as an "Elder" or Big Brother rather than Leading the Way Through the Lower Realms with the Initiated Soul following as was done before This Soul was Established in the Soul Realm or Eternal Life.

It is important to state again that the Soul *always* has Free Will and is free to choose into karma and forfeiture of the Spiritual Worlds gained.

2 Not all karma left behind is to be cleared; some is left behind on all the Levels of the Lower Worlds as it is needed to be in the world and is "pulled up" by The Master when the Initiated Soul leaves the body in what the world mistakenly labels as "death".

ENTRÉE TWO

1 To Hold the Frequency of the Soul Realm is to be able to Vibrate at That Frequency. This means that the Soul has Gained the necessary Spiritual Strength to do so by Its Following *exactly* the Spiritual Instructions Given At The Time

Of Initiation. This involves Focusing on the Godpoint at the Upper Part Of The Third Eye in *Dhyan* while doing *Simran*, the Repetition of the Spiritually Charged Sacred Names Of God.

To Hold the Frequency of the Soul Realm is to have "pushed through" all the Realms below. While this is true for all the Realms in the Lower Worlds the Initiated Soul now has the Spiritual Strength to do What is noted in the previous Endnote and clear the karma left behind—leaving what is necessary to live on this planet—on the Realms below It, Which the Soul is unable to do until Established in This Realm.

2   The Teachings Of The Path Of Soul Transcendence That I am Honored to Bring Forth Focus on Loving the Lord, God by Coming into the Knowing of ourSelves as Soul, as Spirit.

We are not concerned with karma as The Teachings Teach us that by Following *exactly* the Spiritual Instructions Imparted At The Time Of Initiation the various karmas are handled by The Grace Of The Master. The fate karma of an Initiate on This Path is handled in the physical by our going through it in a manner decided by The Master: in a mitigated manner, whether in a dream; through Nighttime Travel or physically. The day-to-day karma—the karma we create in our daily lives—is assigned only to the present life as it cannot be assigned to future ones as stored karma if the Soul is to be Given an Opportunity to Return Home to God; it is handled as determined by The Master. Stored karma—for future lifetimes—is handled by The Master's Grace At The Time Of Initiation for, as stated before, The Master wishes to Give the Initiate the Full Opportunity to Return Home.

The Original Karma—when we were Created as Soul—Completes Itself when the Soul merges back into the Godhead.

The Teachings have no concern or focus upon karma. Our ONLY Focus is on Loving the Lord, God.

3   In the Worlds of Spirit the Soul to be Initiated meets The Master of the One To Whom It Will be Assigned and a Spiritual Contract is entered into; when This Soul incarnates It takes Initiation as per This Contract.

Souls That are not to be Initiated are under the Lords of Karma and their fate karma is agreed upon in the Contract into Which They enter.

All of the above is part of the Beautifully Choreographed Dance Of The Divine in Its March to Completion.

ENTRÉE THREE

1   The Soul's living in These Realms between incarnations is referred to as being in the "bardo" stage in Buddhist and in other eastern thought.

ENTRÉE FOUR

1   The Method Taught At The Time Of Initiation is similar to That originating a few thousand years ago in Northern India and referred to as Nirguna Sampradaya or the Sant Tradition. While the Method is similar the ease of Access to the Spiritual Worlds differs according to the Spiritual Dispensation within Which The Master is working. For a brief discussion of Nirguna Sampradaya see Parrinder, op. cit. 251-254.

ENTRÉE FIVE

1   I have named It the Unipolar Existence as only Spirit exists in the Soul Realm and "above". There is no

density—only Spirit—on These Realms, as karma exists only in the Lower Worlds, Where There is duality.

It is in the Unipolar Existence That the Soul is no longer subject to karma and reincarnation and Continues Its Progression with the Sacred Opportunity to Progress *while in the body* thanks to the Extraordinary Gift of Part II of THE GRAND EXPERIMENT—the New Spiritual Dispensation.

2   "Satsang" means "association" and refers here to being with The Master to hear the Talks imparting The Teachings Of The Path Of Soul Transcendence and to Receive the Upliftment and Upvibration—the many Blessings—of being in the Presence of The Master.

3   The Teacher can be called a Wayshower for the simple reason that The Teacher has shown the Initiated Soul—after Spiritual Charging the Sacred Names Of the Lord, God—how to sit in *Simran* and *Dhyan* and be with the Lord, God as the Lord, God.

"Wayshower" is a very appropriate description for additional reasons as well. The Teacher—in Reality, the Spiritual Form Of The Master—goes ahead of the Initiated Soul in the Inner Worlds with that Soul following and "shows" It the Way until the Soul is Upvibrated to the Soul Realm.

Also, as described in the first Endnote for ENTRÉE ONE, once the Soul has reached and is Established in the Soul Realm It continues Its Journey while also now being able to clear the karma below the Soul Realm as It has gathered the Spiritual Strength to do so. It has Gained the Spiritual Strength because of Its Efforts and the Grace Of The Master and the Knowledge to do so because the Master has "shown" the Initiated Soul how.